TOEFL® MAP

MAP Speaking

New TOEFL® Edition

Intermediate

DARAKWON

TOEFL® MAP Speaking Intermediate

New TOEFL® Edition

Publisher Chung Kyudo
Editor Cho Sangik
Authors Shane Spivey, Jonathan S. McClelland
Designers Park Narae, Jung Kyuok

First published in November 2022
By Darakwon, Inc.
Darakwon Bldg., 211, Munbal-ro, Paju-si, Gyeonggi-do 10881
Republic of Korea
Tel: 82-2-736-2031 (Ext. 250)
Fax: 82-2-732-2037

ISBN 978-89-277-8032-8 14740
      978-89-277-8025-0 14740 (set)

www.darakwon.co.kr

Photo Credits
Shutterstock.com

Components Main Book / Scripts and Answer Key
8 7 6 5 4 3 2   24 25 26 27 28

Introduction

Studying for the TOEFL® iBT is no easy task and is not one that is to be undertaken lightly. It requires a great deal of effort as well as dedication on the part of the student. It is our hope that, by using *TOEFL® Map Speaking Intermediate* as either a textbook or a study guide, the task of studying for the TOEFL® iBT will become somewhat easier for the student and less of a burden.

Students who wish to excel on the TOEFL® iBT must attain a solid grasp of the four important skills in the English language: reading, listening, speaking, and writing. The Darakwon *TOEFL® Map* series covers all four of these skills in separate books. There are also three different levels in all four topics. This book, *TOEFL® Map Speaking Intermediate*, covers the speaking aspect of the test at the intermediate level. With this book, students will be able to listen to lectures and conversations, read academic passages, learn vocabulary and expressions, and study topics that appear on the TOEFL® iBT.

TOEFL® Map Speaking Intermediate has been designed for use in both a classroom setting and as a study guide for individual learners. For this reason, it offers a comprehensive overview of the TOEFL® iBT Speaking section. Particularly, in Part B, learners are presented with passages, lectures, and conversations similar to those on the TOEFL® iBT. The topics presented in this book are based on extensive research of actual test topics. In addition, each task contains exercises and questions that help students learn to mater the skills needed for that task. A sample response is provided for comparison, which helps learners develop a better understanding of how to form their own responses. As students progress through each chapter, they should become more comfortable with each task and eventually develop all of the skills they need to master the TOEFL® iBT.

In addition, *TOEFL® Map Speaking Intermediate* was further designed with all aspects of the student's performance in mind. The material found in these pages can prepare students to approach the TOEFL® iBT confidently and to achieve superior results. However, despite the valuable information within this book, nothing can replace hard work and dedication. In order to get the most benefit from studying *TOEFL® Map Speaking Intermediate*, the student must strive to do his or her best on every task in every chapter. We wish you luck in your study of both English and the TOEFL® iBT, and we hope that you are able to use *TOEFL® Map Speaking Intermediate* to improve your abilities in both.

Shane Spivey
Jonathan S. McClelland

TABLE
OF
CONTENTS

How Is This Book Different?

TOEFL® Map Speaking Intermediate prepares students for success on the TOEFL® iBT with a unique curriculum. Above all, in Part B, students are provided with plenty of activities, exercises, and critical thinking questions. The activities and the exercises for each task are specially designed to develop skills particular to that task. The critical thinking questions will assist students in developing a logical and organized response to each prompt. The sample responses will help students model their own responses, and the guided responses can provide an extra bit of assistance.

The primary emphasis of *TOEFL® Map Speaking Intermediate* is on developing ideas. In order to be successful on the TOEFL, especially on the independent speaking tasks, students must be able to think quickly and use their ideas to develop complete responses. *TOEFL® Map Speaking Intermediate* addresses this need with critical thinking questions and idea webs. The questions help students approach the questions critically, which leads to the formation of ideas for a response. The idea webs allow students to map out their ideas before planning their responses.

Another unique feature of *TOEFL® Map Speaking Intermediate* is that its format provides students with the opportunity to gain an in-depth understanding of each question type. The tasks on the TOEFL® iBT Speaking test can be confusing, but *TOEFL® Map Speaking Intermediate* will give students a deep understanding of each question type. The following unique features of this book, found in Part B, help accomplish that goal.

Warm-up Questions
For the independent speaking task, students are presented with three questions related to the prompt. The questions are designed to help students think about the questions in a way that allows them to form opinions and reasons.

Sample Response
Each task in the book includes a sample response that shows students what a high-scoring response looks like. While this response helps students see the aspects of an ideal response, they should understand that a response can include some errors and still receive a high score.

Focusing
Each integrated task ends with a focus on one of the following skills: stress, pronunciation, viewpoints, and paraphrasing. Each skill is extremely useful for performing well on the TOEFL® iBT.

How to Use
This Book

The exercises and the questions for each task in *TOEFL® Map Speaking Intermediate* have been designed to sharpen individual skills. The material found within these pages will gradually prepare students to master the TOEFL® iBT Speaking test. Part C provides two complete sample tests that are modeled on the actual test. Teachers are encouraged to utilize every aspect of the book. Students should follow the directions presented for each task and skip none of the tasks. This method will provide the most benefit to students in terms of both their speaking and test-taking abilities. Before beginning Part B of the book, teachers may wish to review the TOEFL® iBT Speaking scoring rubric with students. That rubric is provided on page 23. This will give students and teachers a more complete understanding of how to respond to each task.

Part A Understanding Speaking Question Types

This section is designed to make students familiar with the types of questions found on the TOEFL® iBT Speaking test. Each question, called a "task," is explained in a simple and clear way. The purpose is to give students an in-depth understanding of each task. Part A also explains the exercises for each task and how to complete them. It is vital that students and teachers review Part A before completing Part B and Part C.

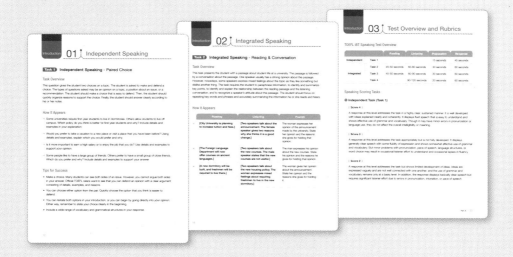

Part B Building Knowledge & Skills for the Speaking Test

Independent Speaking Task 1

The independent task is full of activities to help students think critically and organize their ideas. Students should use this task to develop skills that can be used on the test. The specific exercises are as follows:

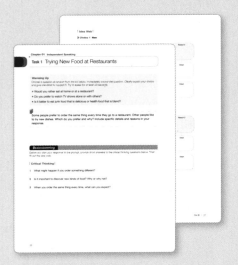

Warming Up

This exercise helps students respond quickly about personal opinions. Students should respond naturally without worrying about the quality of their answers. The goal is to warm up, not to produce a perfect response.

Brainstorming

The first part of this exercise is critical thinking, which helps students approach a question in a way that leads for a response. After answering the question, students can use the idea web to write down their ideas.

Organizing

Students write their brainstorming ideas down in an organized fashion that can be used when giving their responses to the prompt.

Speaking

Students give their responses to the prompt. The guided response can be filled in before answering if students require additional assistance.

Comparing

The high-scoring response lets students hear an example of a response that fulfills all the criteria for a high score. Students should use this response to improve their own scores.

Integrated Speaking Task 2 & 3

In tasks 2 and 3, students are given plenty of exercises to maximize their understanding of the TOEFL® iBT. The exercises are designed not only to promote critical thinking but also to give students the tools they need to master each task. More information on the exercises for tasks 2 and 3 is provided below.

Reading - Analyzing

Students are presented with questions related to the reading passage. The first question helps students paraphrase the key idea or concept in the reading. The second and third questions check reading comprehension. The fourth question reinforces the *TOEFL® Map Speaking Intermediate* emphasis on critical thinking.

Listening - Summarizing

Students are asked to briefly paraphrase the information contained in the listening portion of the integrated task.

Synthesizing

Tasks 2 and 3 ask students to synthesize the information in the reading and listening portions. This exercise is designed to ensure that students have a complete understanding of the information in the task.

Speaking

Students respond to the prompt and can use the guided response if they desire.

Comparing

Students can hear a model response in order to find areas of their own responses that need to be improved.

Focusing

Focusing on Transitions in task 2 gives students the chance to identify and practice transitioning between ideas. This is a basic skill that will benefit students in every task. In Task 3, Focusing on Pronunciation helps students develop this crucial skill. Pronunciation is important on all parts of the TOEFL® iBT Speaking test. Therefore, this section includes words that many students have difficulty pronouncing correctly.

Integrated Speaking Task 4

The goal of task 4 is to briefly summarize a lecture and then to restate the key points about what the lecturer describes. To meet this goal, *TOEFL® Map Speaking Intermediate* provides specific exercises to help students quickly prepare strong responses to the prompt.

Listening - Summarizing

While listening to the lecture, students can take notes in the space provided. The notes are partially completed, but students may add more information if they wish. After listening, students are asked to verbally summarize the lecture. This exercise serves as an effective warm-up activity.

Speaking

Students respond to the prompt by using their organized notes for help. A guided response can be completed before responding for students who wish to focus more on pronunciation and delivery.

Comparing

The sample response shows students how to deliver a strong response to the prompt. It can be used to evaluate students' responses.

Focusing

In task 4, Focusing on Paraphrasing emphasizes using various grammar and vocabulary, which is very important in task 4.

Part C Experiencing the TOEFL iBT Actual Tests

This final portion of the book gives students a chance to experience an actual TOEFL® iBT test. There are two sets of tests that are modeled on the speaking section of the TOEFL® iBT. The questions and the topics are similar to those on the real test. Taking these tests allows students the opportunity to measure their own performance ability on an actual test.

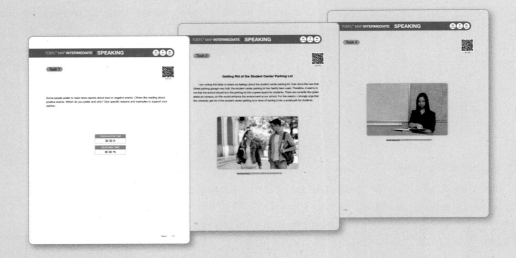

Part **A**

Understanding Speaking Question Types

 # 01 Independent Speaking

Task 1 Independent Speaking - Paired Choice

Task Overview

This question gives the student two choices on a topic. The student is asked to make and defend a choice. The types of questions asked may be an opinion on a topic, a position about an issue, or a recommendation. The student should make a choice that is easy to defend. Then, the student should quickly organize reasons to support the choice. Finally, the student should answer clearly according to his or her notes.

How It Appears

→ Some universities require first-year students to live in dormitories. Others allow students to live off campus. Which policy do you think is better for first-year students and why? Include details and examples in your explanation.

→ Would you prefer to take a vacation to a new place or visit a place that you have been before? Using details and examples, explain which you would prefer and why.

→ Is it more important to earn a high salary or to enjoy the job that you do? Use details and examples to support your opinion.

→ Some people like to have a large group of friends. Others prefer to have a small group of close friends. Which do you prefer and why? Include details and examples to support your answer.

Tips for Success

◆ Make a choice. Many students can see both sides of an issue. However, you cannot argue both sides in your answer. Official TOEFL raters want to see that you can defend an opinion with a clear argument consisting of details, examples, and reasons.

◆ You can choose either option from the pair. Quickly choose the option that you think is easier to defend.

◆ You can restate both options in your introduction, or you can begin by going directly into your opinion. Either way, remember to state your choice clearly in the beginning.

◆ Include a wide range of vocabulary and grammatical structures in your response.

Example of the Task

Question

Do you prefer to play individual sports or team sports? Include details and examples to support your answer.

Preparation time: 15 seconds | Response time: 45 seconds

01-01

Sample Response

Introduction	Although team sports can be exciting, I prefer to participate in individual sports instead.
Detail	When I play an individual sport, I don't have to worry about the performance of my teammates. One sport I love to play is golf. I know that if I win or lose, it's a result of my own actions. Therefore, every game is a chance for me to feel proud of myself if I win or to improve as a player if I lose.
Example	I also prefer individual sports because I think they are usually faster paced. If you play a team sport like baseball or basketball, there are many times when you must wait while others hit the ball or try to score. In an individual sport like tennis, there is almost no time spent waiting.

Explanation

A four-point response to the first task should be one that clearly takes a side and defends it well. In this task, the student is asked to give an opinion about an issue. The sample response begins with a thesis statement that directly states the speaker's opinion. The two supporting details are not mentioned in the introduction. This allows the speaker to give a more detailed response within the given time. The response is broken down into two supporting reasons, and each reason is explained with a relevant example.

Task 2 Integrated Speaking - Reading & Conversation

Task Overview

This task presents the student with a passage about student life at a university. The passage is followed by a conversation about the passage. One speaker usually has a strong opinion about the passage. However, nowadays, some speakers express mixed feelings about the topic as they like something but dislike another thing. The task requires the student to paraphrase information, to identify and summarize key points, to identify and explain the relationship between the reading passage and the listening conversation, and to recognize a speaker's attitude about the passage. The student should focus on repeating key words and phrases and accurately summarizing the information he or she reads and hears.

How It Appears

	Reading	Listening	Prompt
→	[City University is planning to increase tuition and fees.]	[Two speakers talk about the announcement. The female speaker gives two reasons why she thinks it is a good change.]	The woman expresses her opinion of the announcement made by the university. State her opinion and the reasons she gives for holding that opinion.
→	[The Foreign Language Department will now offer courses on ancient languages.]	[Two speakers talk about the new courses. The male speaker states that the new courses are not useful.]	The man expresses his opinion about the new courses. State his opinion and the reasons he gives for holding that opinion.
→	[A new dormitory will be built, and freshmen will be required to live there.]	[Two speakers talk about the new housing policy. The woman expresses mixed feelings about requiring freshmen to live in the new dormitory.]	The woman gives her opinion about the announcement. State her opinion and the reasons she gives for holding it.

Tips for Success

◆ You are allowed 45 seconds to read the passage. Read it quickly once, and then read it again to note the important details.

◆ As you listen to the conversation, take notes on both speakers' opinions. You will not know which speaker's opinion you must speak about until after the conversation.

◆ The speaker with the longest speaking segments is usually the speaker whose opinion you need to summarize.

◆ The task asks you to show that you can synthesize the reading and listening portions. To do this, refer to the information from the reading passage as you state the speaker's opinion.

Example of the Task

✪ Reading

A dance team is starting a dance class on a college campus, so it is inviting students to join. Read the announcement from the dance team. You will have 45 seconds to read the announcement. Begin reading now.

Happy Toes Dance Class

　　Attention, all students who want to get in shape and have fun. The Happy Toes Dance Team is offering evening dance classes beginning on September 5. We will learn all kinds of dance methods from swing dancing to jazz dancing. Anyone who is interested is welcome to join the fun. We meet at Carter Hall every evening at 6:30 PM. Be sure to wear comfortable clothes and to bring your dancing shoes. As a special offer, the first week of classes will be free. We hope to see you there.

Happy Toes Dance Team

✪ Listening

Now listen to two students as they discuss the announcement.

01-02

W: This looks like something I would be interested in.

M: I didn't know that you were interested in dancing. Have you always been a dancer?

W: No, I actually don't know the first thing about dancing.

M: So why would you want to join a dance class? Are you trying to expand your interests?

W: That's not exactly it. I told you I wanted to lose ten pounds this semester. I've been jogging, but it isn't very much fun.

M: You're right. Jogging can be really boring.

W: But dancing would be fun. It's also good exercise, but it is more interesting than just running around in circles.

M: That's a terrific idea. I think this will help you get into shape. But what if you commit to the class and it turns out that you don't like it? Dancing isn't for everyone.

W: What do I have to lose? The first week of classes is free. If I don't like it, I can quit after the first week.

M: And then you haven't wasted any money, and you will know that the class isn't right for you.

W: Exactly. I think this will work out perfectly for me.

✪ Question

The woman gives her opinion about the dance classes advertised in the announcement. State her opinion and the reasons she gives for her opinion.

Preparation time: 30 seconds | Response time: 60 seconds

01-03

✪ Sample Response

Introduction	The woman is giving her opinion about the evening dance class. She thinks the class is a good idea because it will help her get in shape and it is free to try.
Detail	The female student begins by saying that she wants to lose ten pounds. She has been jogging, but it is boring to her. She says that dancing is good exercise and a lot more interesting than jogging. Even though she is not a dancer, she thinks it would be a good way to get in shape.
Example	She then responds to the man's question about committing to a class. She points out that the first week is free. Because of this, she can try out the class and see if dancing is for her. If she doesn't like it, she can quit. That way, she can explore a new exercising option without making a big commitment.

✪ Explanation

The second task requires that the student understand one speaker's opinion in relation to the reading passage. This requires the student to summarize and to paraphrase. The sample response begins by explaining a basic summary of the woman's opinion and her reasons for it. It then moves on to more detailed explanations. The speaker uses good transitions to move between thoughts. The level of vocabulary is appropriate for the task, and the speaker uses key words and phrases from the passage ("get in shape" and "dancing is for her"). Overall, the speaker clearly summarizes the woman's opinion and the reasons for her opinion in a well-organized manner.

Task 3 Integrated Speaking - Reading & Lecture

Task Overview

This task focuses on an academic topic. Students first read a short passage that gives general information about the topic. Then, students listen to part of a lecture, which gives details and examples of the topic. Students should take notes while listening and then write down the key words and ideas from the lecture. The task tests students' abilities to summarize key points, to explain the relationship between the reading passage and the listening lecture, and to explain how concrete examples explain more general ideas.

How It Appears

Reading	Listening	Prompt
[Advertising – Brief explanation of the purpose of advertising]	[The lecture explains two methods of advertising.]	The professor explains two types of advertising. Describe how these examples explain why businesses use advertisements.
[Psychology – A description of how personality can affect one's career choice]	[The professor describes a personality type and the job that best suits it.]	The professor discusses why people who are quiet may become great actors. Describe the personality type and why it is suited for acting.
[Animal Science – A summary of animal playing habits]	[The lecture describes how chimpanzees can learn to play tag.]	The professor explains how chimpanzees demonstrate the ability for animals to play. Describe how chimpanzees play and how this relates to animals in general.

Tips for Success

◆ Take notes on the main idea and any important details while you read.

◆ The reading passage expresses a general concept in non-concrete terms. Be prepared for the lecture to present concrete examples to illustrate the concept.

◆ Listen for transition words in the lecture. These will help you organize your notes.

Example of the Task

✪ Reading

Now read a passage about ergonomics. You have 45 seconds to read the passage. Begin reading now.

Ergonomics

Some inventions do not create new products or designs. Instead, they improve upon existing products. Ergonomics is the science of improving workplace equipment through redesign. In the past, office equipment was designed to be functional. It may not have been very comfortable to use, however, and it may not have been the most efficient design. Ergonomics does not attempt to create new and innovative types of equipment. It simply looks for ways to redesign office equipment to make it both easier to use and more efficient.

✪ Listening

Now listen to part of a lecture on this topic in a business class.

Professor (Female)

01-04

Ergonomics is a hot topic in business these days. I suppose the reason is that modern people spend so much time working indoors and that ergonomics usually focuses on office equipment.

You've probably heard the word "ergonomics" several times in the past, but how does it work in everyday life? I'll give you an example of how it affects my life personally. In my office here at the university, I often participate in meetings over the phone. It's important that I am not only able to sit comfortably for one or two hours on the phone but also that I can work while doing so. A regular handheld telephone receiver is not very ergonomic in that sense. Thankfully, someone had the great idea to buy headsets for the staff in the Business Department. Now, when I am on the phone for hours at a time, I can comfortably sit and listen to the meeting. Not only that, but both of my hands are also free to take notes or to do other tasks. It really is a simple ergonomic concept.

✪ Question

The professor explains how ergonomic design is used in the workplace. Explain the concept of ergonomics and how the example given in the lecture illustrates this concept.

Preparation time: 30 seconds | Response time: 60 seconds

01-05

⭐ Sample Response

Introduction	Ergonomics is the study of making office equipment easier to use and more efficient. It is mostly used in the workplace. It does not innovate new concepts but instead focuses on redesigning office equipment that is already in use.
Detail 1	The professor talks about how ergonomics can be seen in her own personal life. She explains that she often participates in lengthy meetings on the phone. A regular phone can be uncomfortable to hold. So her department purchased headsets for the staff.
Detail 2	The professor describes the headset as a basic ergonomic design. The goal of ergonomics is to make equipment more comfortable to use and to increase efficiency. The headset is more comfortable than the handheld phone because the professor does not have to hold it. It also allows her to work more efficiently by freeing up her hand.

⭐ Explanation

The goal of the third task is to show that students are able to synthesize material from written and spoken sources. Student responses must accurately convey important information from both sources. In the sample response, the student first summarizes the concept in the reading passage: ergonomics. The student gives a brief and clear description of what ergonomics is and is not. The response moves on to the example by explaining how and why ergonomics was used in the professor's office. Finally, the example is linked with the concept by stating how the example demonstrates both key characteristics of ergonomics.

Task 4 Integrated Speaking - Lecture

Task Overview

This task involves listening to part of a lecture about an academic topic. The topics are from any major field of study, such as psychology or business. However, the lecture focuses on a detailed part of that field. The passage does not require students to know anything about the topic beforehand, but it does require an advanced vocabulary. When giving their responses, students should demonstrate that they are able to summarize the key points from the lecture and accurately explain the connection between the general ideas and concrete examples in the lecture.

How It Appears

Listening	Prompt
→ [Lecture about the causes of the Mexican-American War]	Using points and examples from the lecture, explain how American involvement in northern Mexico led to the Mexican-American War.
→ [Lecture giving information about the history of fashion]	Using points and examples from the lecture, explain how fashion began in ancient societies.
→ [An explanation about the Impressionist Movement in art]	Using points and examples from the lecture, explain how the Impressionist Movement began and how it affected the art world.

Tips for Success

◆ Listen for words that the professor emphasizes as well as any technical terms and vocabulary. Write them down and include them in your summary.

◆ Organize your notes into two sections: main idea and details. While listening, write down any words that you feel are key words that you should include in your response.

◆ Many students have difficulty with accurately and completely presenting facts in this task. To succeed, you must develop strong note-taking skills. Abbreviate long words and use mathematical symbols to replace transition words.

◆ The professor will not always give strong signal words to separate ideas. As you listen, take organized notes and establish the lecture's organization as you listen.

Example of the Task

✪ Listening

Now listen to part of a lecture in a zoology class.

01-06

Professor (Male)

Many of us watch nature shows, and we see young animals playing. It is cute to watch the lion cubs fight or the baby birds fly around. This may look like simple behavior, but it is not just for fun. As a matter of fact, this playing increases an animal's chance at survival as an adult.

Let's look at lion cubs. When they are young, they like to wrestle around and fight with one another. It may look like they are angry, but they are just playing. Sometimes the playing can get rather rough. Later in life, they will have to hunt for food. They will need to have strong muscles and speed. Thanks to all of their playing as cubs, they have the skills to chase down, attack, and kill other animals. This increases their chances of survival because it equips them to find food in their adult lives.

If you ever watch young monkeys playing, you'll notice one thing: They like to move around a lot. They swing from tree to tree and from branch to branch. They chase one another around while playing a monkey version of the game tag. Again, this is more than just playing. There will come a time in their lives when they must escape danger. Perhaps there is a dangerous snake or an angry tiger nearby. The monkey is going to need to escape quickly. All of that practice as a youngster when it was playing with its friends should have prepared the monkey to run away and avoid danger.

✪ Question

The professor explains the purpose of play among young animals. Using points and examples from the lecture, explain how play increases animals' chances of survival.

01-07

Preparation time: 20 seconds | Response time: 60 seconds

✪ Sample Response

Introduction	The professor explains how, when young animals play, they are doing more than just playing. They are actually preparing for their adult lives. Their playing activities develop useful survival skills for later. The professor makes this point by giving two examples of animal play.
Detail 1	First, the professor explains that lion cubs enjoy play fighting with one another. They are young and do not have to hunt, but later in their lives, they will need to be able to catch their food. When they are playing together as cubs, the lions are building their muscles and learning how to attack. Without these basic hunting skills, they would probably not be able to survive.

| Detail 2 | Second, the professor describes how playing can develop defense skills. He talks about young monkeys swinging in trees. They practice chasing one another around and moving quickly through the trees all the time. This increases their chances of survival because it allows them to escape danger later on in their lives, such as when they are being chased by dangerous animals like tigers. |

✪ Explanation

The fourth task calls on students to summarize the information in a lecture. Students must be sure to repeat the information as accurately and completely as possible. The sample response briefly summarizes the topic of the lecture and then moves on to explain the two examples that the professor gives. The speaker uses clear and basic transitions ("first" and "second") to move between the two examples. She uses a mixture of grammatical forms and incorporates vocabulary from the lecture ("cubs" and "swing"). While summarizing each example, the speaker explains how the example ties in with the main argument, which is that animal play increases survivability.

03 Test Overview and Rubrics

TOEFL iBT Speaking Test Overview

		Reading	Listening	Preparation	Response
Independent	Task 1			15 seconds	45 seconds
Integrated	Task 2	45-50 seconds	60-80 seconds	30 seconds	60 seconds
	Task 3	45-50 seconds	60-90 seconds	30 seconds	60 seconds
	Task 4		90-120 seconds	20 seconds	60 seconds

Speaking Scoring Tasks

❶ Independent Task (Task 1)

| Score 4 |

A response at this level addresses the task in a highly clear, sustained manner. It is well developed with ideas explained clearly and coherently. It displays fluid speech that is easy to understand and shows effective use of grammar and vocabulary. Though it may have minor errors in pronunciation or language use, they do not affect the overall intelligibility or meaning.

| Score 3 |

A response at this level addresses the task appropriately but is not fully developed. It displays generally clear speech with some fluidity of expression and shows somewhat effective use of grammar and vocabulary. But minor problems with pronunciation, pace of speech, language structures, or word choice may result in occasional listener effort to understand and occasional lapses in fluency.

| Score 2 |

A response at this level addresses the task but shows limited development of ideas. Ideas are expressed vaguely and are not well connected with one another, and the use of grammar and vocabulary remains only at a basic level. In addition, the response displays basically clear speech but requires significant listener effort due to errors in pronunciation, intonation, or pace of speech.

| Score 1 |

A response at this level is very short and practically not related to the task. It lacks substance beyond the expression of very basic ideas and is hard for the listener to understand due to consistent pronunciation, stress, and intonation problems and a severely limited control of grammar and vocabulary.

| Score 0 |

A response at this level is not relevant to the task or has no substance.

❷ Integrated Tasks (Tasks 2-4)

| Score 4 |

A response at this level effectively addresses the task by presenting the necessary information and appropriate details. It generally shows clear, fluid, sustained speech and effective control of grammar and vocabulary. Though it may have minor errors in pronunciation, intonation, or language use, they do not affect the overall intelligibility or meaning.

| Score 3 |

A response at this level addresses the task appropriately but is not fully developed. It conveys the necessary information but does not include sufficient details. It shows generally clear speech with some fluidity of expression, but minor problems with pronunciation, intonation, or pacing may result in some listener effort. It also displays somewhat effective use of grammar and vocabulary despite the existence of some incorrect word choice or language structures.

| Score 2 |

A response at this level conveys some relevant information, but the ideas are not well connected. It omits key ideas, shows limited development, or exhibits a misunderstanding of key ideas. It shows clear speech occasionally but mostly demonstrates difficulties with pronunciation, intonation, or pace of speech—problems that require significant listener effort. It also displays only a basic level of grammar and vocabulary, which results in a limited or vague expression of ideas or unclear connections.

| Score 1 |

A response at this level is very short and practically not related to the task. It fails to provide much relevant content and contains inaccurate or vague expressions of ideas. It is characterized by fragmented speech with frequent pauses and hesitations and consistent pronunciation and intonation problems. It also shows a severely limited range and control of grammar and vocabulary.

| Score 0 |

A response at this level is not relevant to the task or has no substance.

Part B

Building Knowledge & Skills for the Speaking Test

Task 1 Trying New Food at Restaurants

Warming Up

Choose a question at random from the list below. Immediately answer the question. Clearly explain your choice and give one detail to support it. Try to speak for at least 20 seconds.

- Would you rather eat at home or at a restaurant?

- Do you prefer to watch TV shows alone or with others?

- Is it better to eat junk food that is delicious or healthy food that is bland?

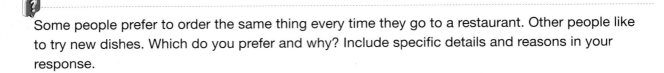

Some people prefer to order the same thing every time they go to a restaurant. Other people like to try new dishes. Which do you prefer and why? Include specific details and reasons in your response.

Brainstorming

Before you plan your response to the prompt, provide short answers to the critical thinking questions below. Then, fill out the idea web.

| Critical Thinking |

1   What might happen if you order something different?

2   Is it important to discover new kinds of food? Why or why not?

3   When you order the same thing every time, what can you expect?

| Idea Web |

▶ Choice 1 New

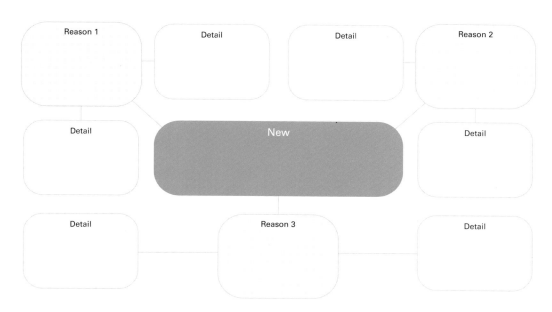

▶ Choice 2 Different

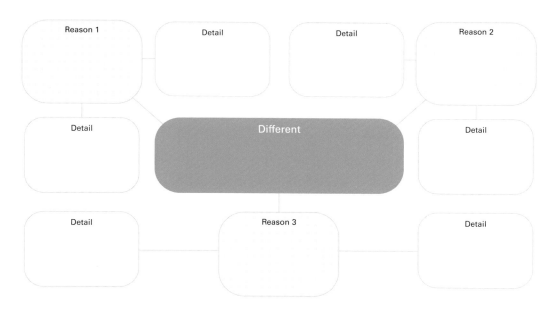

Organizing

Use your answers to the critical thinking questions and the idea web to organize your response.

My Choice:

Reason 1:

Reason 2:

Speaking

Now give your spoken response for 45 seconds. You may use the guided response below to assist you.

▶ **Guided Response 1 Order the Same Dish**

When I go to restaurants, I usually order _____ . There are a couple of reasons why I _____ . For one thing, ordering _____ lets me _____ . Because I have ordered it before, I know that _____ . The other reason is that when I try new food, it makes me feel _____ . The dish might be delicious, or it might be disgusting, so _____ . That's why I always order _____ when I go to restaurants.

▶ **Guided Response 2 Order a New Dish**

I don't eat out often, so whenever I go out, I want to _____ . The main reason is that I can _____ . When you order the same thing, it is always _____ . But a new dish can be _____ . That makes eating out _____ than usual. In addition to that, I think that ordering a new dish _____ . I can learn about _____ , and I can expand my _____ . So just by eating food, I can _____ .

| **Comparing** | Listen to a sample response and compare it with yours.

Order the
Same Dish

Order a
New Dish

02-01

02-02

Read the following questions related to the topic. For question 1, use the information provided to make responses. For questions 2 to 6, use your own ideas to make responses.

1   Schools need to teach students how to prepare healthy meals.

Agree	Disagree
- can teach students a valuable skill - lets students learn about nutrition and good health	- not an academic subject → shouldn't be taught at school - parents should teach their children how to cook

2   People in the past ate healthier and more nutritious food than people do today.

Agree	Disagree

3   Everyone should be able to cook a few simple meals.

Agree	Disagree

4   Some people prefer to cook their meals at home. Other people prefer to eat out at restaurants. Which do you prefer and why?

Cook Meals at Home	Eat Out at Restaurants

5   Some people prefer to try food from foreign countries. Other people prefer to eat only food from their own country. Which do you prefer and why?

Food from Foreign Countries	Food from One's Own Country

6   Some people prefer to make home-cooked meals. Other people prefer to eat prepared meals. Which do you prefer and why?

Home-Cooked Meals	Prepared Meal

Task 2 Campus Sailing Club

● Vocabulary   Take a few moments to review the vocabulary items that will appear in this task.

proximity *n.* the state of being near something

put one's skills to the test *exp.* to use newly learned abilities

dues *n.* money owed for membership in a group or club

expand one's horizons *exp.* to try something new

skipper *n.* the master of a boat or ship

bargain *n.* a good price

debt *n.* the state of owing money

Reading

Read the following announcement from a club at a university.

City University Sailing Club

All students with an interest in water sports are invited to join the Full Sails Sailing Club. Whether you were raised on a boat or have never been near water, the Full Sails Sailing Club is a great way to make friends and to live life to the fullest. With City University's proximity to Lake Viola, we have easy access to water. We meet two Saturdays a month to learn about sailing and to put our skills to the test. Dues are only 130 dollars per semester. This covers the costs of equipment and space at the harbor. Expand your horizons and join today.

| Analyzing | Answer the following questions. Give brief spoken responses to questions 2-4.

1 What is the purpose of the announcement?

   Ⓐ To promote a student club

   Ⓑ To encourage water sports

   Ⓒ To criticize sailing

   Ⓓ To educate club members

2 Why does the announcement mention the university's proximity to a lake?

3 How much does it cost money to join, and how is the money used?

4 **Critical Thinking:** Why would someone want to join a sailing club?

Listen to a short conversation related to the reading. Take notes about the man's opinion.

Notes

The man is _____ in the announcement.

Reason 1   *wants to try new things; loves*

02-03

Reason 2

Key Words and Details

| Summarizing | In your own words, explain the man's opinion about the announcement.

Give a brief spoken response to the questions based on the announcement and the conversation.

1   Why does the man say that he has found the club he wants to join this year?

2   What is the woman's reaction to the announcement?

3   How would the man need to change his lifestyle in order to join the club?

Now give your spoken response for 60 seconds. You may use the guided response below to assist you.

The man expresses his opinion about the sailing club. Explain his opinion and the reasons he gives for holding it.

▶ **Guided Response**

The speakers are discussing _____. According to the announcement, _____. The man is interested _____ and says _____. His first reason for having that opinion is _____. The woman reminds him that _____, and he says _____.

He then addresses _____. Joining the club would mean he wouldn't be able to _____. He thinks he could _____ and _____.

That way, he could enjoy _____. So he is considering _____ because he wants to _____ and he thinks it will help him _____.

| Comparing | Listen to a sample response and compare it with yours.

02-04

FOCUSING ON TRANSITIONS

Underline all the transition words and phrases used in the sample response. Write them in the space below and practice saying them with natural intonation.

- _____
- _____
- _____
- _____

Task 3 Psychology: Memory Tricks

🎧 **Vocabulary** Take a few moments to review the vocabulary items that will appear in this task.

facts and figures *exp.* exact information about dates, numbers, and other data

recall *n.* the act of remembering something

retention *n.* the ability to hold on to something

eager *adj.* showing strong interest

stuck in one's head *exp.* unable to forget

adversary *n.* an enemy; one who opposes

abolish *v.* to erase permanently; to get rid of

tricky *adj.* confusing; requiring caution and skill

Reading

Read the following passage about memory tricks.

Mnemonic Devices

Most academic subjects require students to memorize facts and figures for recall on examinations. A small percentage of students can easily digest a large number of facts, but the majority of people have a lower rate of retention. In order to boost one's memorization ability, education experts have developed strategies called mnemonic devices. These are tricks that students can use when studying to increase their chances of remembering important information. An eager student should learn a handful of mnemonic devices to use while studying.

| **Analyzing** | Answer the following questions. Give brief spoken responses to questions 2-4.

1   What problem does the passage address?

    Ⓐ Student eagerness

    Ⓑ Understanding facts and figures

    Ⓒ Retention and recall

    Ⓓ Education strategies

2   What is a mnemonic device?

3   According to the passage, why should students learn mnemonic devices?

4   **Critical Thinking:** Why is it sometimes difficult to memorize lists of information?

Listen to a short lecture related to the reading. Take notes on key words and specific information from the lecture.

> **Notes**
>
> **Topic** *mnemonic*   *and how they can be used for*
>
> **Detail 1** *first device = rhyming*
>
> **Detail 2**
>
> **Key Words and Details** *in 1492, silly rhyme, enemy,*

02-05

| **Summarizing** | In your own words, restate the main idea and the key points of the lecture.

Synthesizing

Give a brief spoken response to the questions based on the reading passage and the lecture.

1 How does the professor explain the information in the reading passage?

2 How does the information given in the lecture clarify the information in the reading passage?

3 Why does the professor give examples of some specific mnemonic devices?

Now give your spoken response for 60 seconds. You may use the guided response below to assist you.

The professor explains mnemonic devices by giving two examples. Explain the examples and how they illustrate the concept of mnemonic devices.

▶ Guided Response

The topic of the reading is _____ . These are _____ . According to the passage, using a mnemonic device helps students _____ . The professor elaborates on the topic by _____ . The first one he talks about is _____ . By creating sentences that rhyme, _____ . He gives the example of " _____ ." The professor then introduces a second mnemonic device: _____ . He explains that _____ can help you _____ . The example he uses is for the word " _____ ." Since it sounds like " _____ " and means _____ , he says to picture someone _____ .

| **Comparing** | Listen to a sample response and compare it with yours.

02-06

(**FOCUSING ON PRONUNCIATION**)

Circle five words in the sample response that you have difficulty pronouncing. Write them in the space below. Practice saying these words in a North American accent.

1 _____   2 _____   3 _____

4 _____   5 _____

Task 4 Life Science: Mimicry

🔊 Vocabulary Take a few moments to review the vocabulary items that will appear in this task.

adapt *v.* to adjust based on a situation or environment

evolve *v.* to develop and change over time

mechanism *n.* a method or process for doing something

predator *n.* an animal that hunts another for food

species *n.* a specific group of organisms

attract *v.* to cause to come near; to bring close

snap *v.* to close quickly and forcefully

consume *v.* to eat

Listening

Listen to a lecture on the topic of mimicry. Take notes on key words and concepts in the lecture.

Notes

Topic   *mimicry = animal or plant evolving to*

Detail 1   *defensive mimicry = weak animal looking like*

ex: plain tiger butterfly;

Detail 2

Key Words   *defensive mechanism, weak animal,*

02-07

| **Summarizing** | Using your own words, summarize the topic of the lecture, describe how the professor explains the topic, and restate the key points.

Now give your spoken response for 60 seconds. You may use the guided response below to assist you.

Using points and examples from the lecture, explain how plants and animals use mimicry to adapt to their environment.

▶ Guided Response

The topic of the _____ . This is something that _____

have evolved over time. It is a way for them to _____ . The professor

explains that mimicry works in two ways. One way is _____

predators. This point is illustrated with the example of _____ . According to the lecture, the

butterfly known as the _____ is not _____ because

of _____ . Because of this, butterflies that look like the plain

tiger _____ . Mimicry helps them _____ . The other

way mimicry works is to help predators _____ . This is also explained with an

example: _____ . The Venus flytrap opens _____ , so

some creatures _____ . The creature is _____ , and the

_____ .

| Comparing | Listen to a sample response and compare it with yours.

02-08

⌐ FOCUSING ON PARAPHRASING ⌐

Underline any three sentences in the sample response. Paraphrase each sentence in the space below. Then, practice saying each sentence with natural intonation.

-
-
-

Part **B**

Task 1 Ability vs. Hard Work

Warming Up

Choose a question at random from the list below. Immediately answer the question. Clearly explain your choice and give one detail to support it. Try to speak for at least 20 seconds.

- Do you agree or disagree that entertainers are important to society? Why?

- Is it better to read for pleasure or for learning?

- Is it wise or foolish to learn a skill that does not promote financial success?

Which is more important for becoming a successful writer, musician, or artist: natural ability or hard work? Include specific details and reasons in your response.

Brainstorming

Before you plan your response to the prompt, provide short answers to the critical thinking questions below. Then, fill out the idea web.

| Critical Thinking |

1   How do people learn to sing, play instruments, paint, or do other artistic endeavors?

2   Think of a successful artist. Did that person have training?

3   If you have no natural ability at playing the piano, should you choose another instrument to learn?

| Idea Web |

▶ Choice 1 Innate Ability

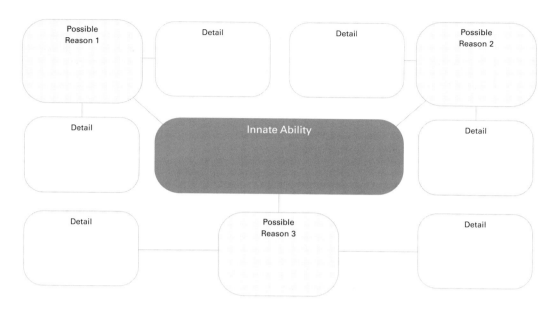

▶ Choice 2 Hard Work

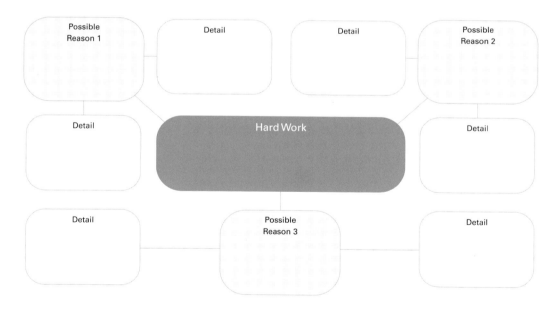

Organizing

Use your answers to the critical thinking questions and the idea web to organize your response.

My Choice:

Reason 1:

Reason 2:

Speaking

Now give your spoken response for 45 seconds. You may use the guided response below to assist you.

▶ Guided Response 1 Natural Ability

Hard work is important for any profession, but I think ＿＿＿＿＿＿＿＿＿. Every person is born with ＿＿＿＿＿＿＿＿. Successful artists are ＿＿＿＿＿＿＿＿ who have found a ＿＿＿＿＿＿＿＿ and developed into a career. Sure, they may have trained, but without ＿＿＿＿＿＿＿＿. Furthermore, if someone has no natural ability, that person will probably ＿＿＿＿＿＿＿＿ instead of continuing it. People like to learn skills that ＿＿＿＿＿＿＿＿. For example, I tried to learn ＿＿＿＿＿＿＿＿. I was terrible even after taking lessons, so ＿＿＿＿＿＿＿＿ and decided to practice ＿＿＿＿＿＿＿＿ instead.

▶ Guided Response 2 Hard Work

When it comes to being a successful artist, I think that ＿＿＿＿＿＿＿＿. One way to prove this is to look at ＿＿＿＿＿＿＿＿ as an example. ＿＿＿＿＿＿＿＿ a successful artist during ＿＿＿＿＿＿＿＿. This artist may have been born with skill, but ＿＿＿＿＿＿＿＿. Without this training, ＿＿＿＿＿＿＿＿. To look at a broader example, there are ＿＿＿＿＿＿＿＿ for all fields of art. These have existed for ＿＿＿＿＿＿＿＿. This shows that, historically, people think that artists ＿＿＿＿＿＿＿＿. In other words, natural ability alone cannot ＿＿＿＿＿＿＿＿.

| Comparing | Listen to a sample response and compare it with yours.

Natural Ability　　Hard Work

02-09　　02-10

Read the following questions related to the topic. For question 1, use the information provided to make responses. For questions 2 to 6, use your own ideas to make responses.

1 Which would you prefer, to have a job that pays well but that requires a lot of work or to have a job that pays poorly but does not require much work?

A Job That Pays Well	A Job That Pays Poorly
- want to make a lot of money - can become successful by working hard	- do not want to work very hard - have few needs so do not have to earn a lot

2 Which is more necessary to have a successful future, a degree from a top college or a good work ethic?

A Degree from a Top College	A Good Work Ethic

3 Only people who work hard can be successful.

Agree	Disagree

4 It is better to have natural talent than to be a hard worker.

Agree	Disagree

5 Modern technology has made it easier for people to become successful.

Agree	Disagree

6 A person with little natural ability can become a talented artist by working hard.

Agree	Disagree

Task 2 Campus Clean-up Day

🔊 Vocabulary Take a few moments to review the vocabulary items that will appear in this task.

cigarette butt *n.* the leftover portion of a used cigarette

turnoff *n.* something that causes dislike or disinterest

potential *adj.* possible

do one's part *exp.* to participate equally

filthy *adj.* extremely dirty

differ *v.* to be different from

enroll *v.* to join, especially a school or university

Reading

Read the following letter to a student newspaper.

Letter to the Editor

Lately, when I walk around campus, all I can see is litter everywhere. Cigarette butts and empty soda cans are casually tossed on the ground by students. The university grounds are beginning to look like a garbage dump. Not only is this a turnoff for current students, but it may also discourage potential students who tour the campus. I think the student body needs to do something about it. I propose that the student government organize a campus clean-up day. All the students should get together and do their part to keep our university beautiful.

Sincerely,
Lindsay Morgan, Junior

| Analyzing | Answer the following questions. Give brief spoken responses to questions 2-4.

1 What is the purpose of the letter?
- Ⓐ To praise the school for having a beautiful campus
- Ⓑ To criticize students who throw garbage on the ground
- Ⓒ To announce a clean-up day to the university's students
- Ⓓ To suggest a solution to a problem affecting the university

2 Why does the letter mention cigarette butts and empty soda cans?

3 How does the writer suggest fixing the stated problem?

4 **Critical Thinking:** Why might students disagree with the writer's suggestion?

Listen to a short conversation related to the reading. Take notes about the woman's opinion.

Notes

The woman _____ with the letter.

Reason 1   *thinks students should focus on*

Reason 2

Key Words and Details   *opinions differ, focus, concentrate,*

02-11

| **Summarizing** | In your own words, explain the woman's opinion about the letter.

Synthesizing

Give a brief spoken response to the questions based on the letter and the conversation.

1   What part of the letter to the editor does the woman agree with?

2   Why does the woman not want to help?

3   How does the man show that he agrees with the woman at the end of the conversation?

Now give your spoken response for 60 seconds. You may use the guided response below to assist you.

The woman expresses her opinion about the campus clean-up day. Explain her opinion and the reasons she gives for holding it.

▶ **Guided Response**

The man and the woman are talking about _____ that addresses the problem of

_____ . The letter writer is upset about _____ . She points to

_____ as examples of the litter that can be found on campus and argues that students

_____ . The woman sees the letter and _____ , but she does not

agree with _____ . She does not feel that students _____ . She

says that a student's goal is _____ , not _____ .

Instead, she argues, the university should _____ . These people

would _____ since they are professionals, and their work would allow students to

_____ .

| Comparing | Listen to a sample response and compare it with yours.

02-12

FOCUSING ON TRANSITIONS

Underline all the transition words and phrases used in the sample response. Write them in the space below and practice saying them with natural intonation.

- _____   • _____

- _____   • _____

Task 3 Plant Biology: Self-Defense

🔊 **Vocabulary** Take a few moments to review the vocabulary items that will appear in this task.

deter *v.* to cause to avoid; to discourage action

herbivorous *adj.* plant-eating

injure *v.* to cause serious pain or damage

whereas *conj.* while at the same time; on the other hand

pesticide *n.* a chemical that kills certain insects

ingest *v.* to swallow and absorb

thorn *n.* a sharp, pointy part of a plant's stem

armor *n.* a hard, protective layer

Reading

Read the following passage about the self-defense of plants.

Self-Defense Mechanisms of Plants

Like animals, plants must adapt to their surroundings in order to survive. The plants we see today are those that evolved mechanisms to deter predators. In the case of plants, predators consist primarily of insects but also herbivorous mammals and birds. There are two main types of plant self-defense: chemical and mechanical. Chemical defense occurs through the production of a chemical that in some way hurts or discomforts predators that eat the plant. Mechanical defense is a physical change the plant evolves that can injure or kill an attacker.

| Analyzing | Answer the following questions. Give brief spoken responses to questions 2-4.

1 What is the purpose of the passage?
- (A) To protect plants from attackers
- (B) To describe how plants avoid being eaten
- (C) To show the difference between two types of self-defense
- (D) To compare the plants of today with ancient plants

2 How does the passage explain the topic?

3 According to the passage, how do chemical and mechanical defenses differ?

4 **Critical Thinking:** Why do different plants evolve different defense mechanisms?

Listen to a short lecture related to the reading. Take notes on key words and specific information from the lecture.

> **Notes**
>
> **Topic** *plants that use self-defense to*
>
> **Detail 1** *chemical defense = the production of*
>
>   *ex: tobacco plant*
>
> **Detail 2**
>
> **Key Words** *physical defense, tobacco,*

02-13

| **Summarizing** | In your own words, restate the main idea and the key points of the lecture.

Give a brief spoken response to the questions based on the reading passage and the lecture.

1 How does the professor explain the information in the reading passage?

2 How does the information given in the lecture clarify the information in the reading passage?

3 Why does the professor mention the defense mechanisms of animals?

Now give your spoken response for 60 seconds. You may use the guided response below to assist you.

The professor explains self-defense mechanisms of plants by giving three examples. Explain the examples and how they illustrate the mechanisms of self-defense used by plants.

▶ Guided Response

The professor begins the lecture by comparing _____. She says that, like animals, plants have evolved _____. She explains with the first example of _____. These plants have _____ that want to eat them. However, because of _____, predators _____. They _____ if they ate the plants. This example _____ the concept of _____ introduced in the reading passage. The professor then brings up _____. The reading passage says that this is _____ used by plants. One example the professor gives is of _____. These grow _____, which, if eaten, _____. Because of that, predators _____. Another example of _____ is the _____, which grows _____ in order to protect its fruit. It is almost impossible for predators to _____.

| **Comparing** | Listen to a sample response and compare it with yours.

02-14

FOCUSING ON PRONUNCIATION

Circle five words in the sample response that you have difficulty pronouncing. Write them in the space below. Practice saying these words in a North American accent.

1 _____   2 _____   3 _____

4 _____   5 _____

Task 4 Business: Lateral Thinking

🔊 **Vocabulary** Take a few moments to review the vocabulary items that will appear in this task.

logic *n.* a systematic way of thinking to solve problems

desired *adj.* wanted; hoped for

outcome *n.* a result

lateral *adj.* moving sideways; horizontal

staff *n.* the employees working at a company

budget *n.* a plan for the use of money

session *n.* a time period used for a specific purpose

housekeeper *n.* a person who cleans rooms, especially at a hotel

Listening

Listen to a lecture on the topic of lateral thinking. Take notes on key words and concepts in the lecture.

> **Notes**
>
> Topic   *lateral thinking =*
>
> Detail 1   *happens by using creativity and*
>
> *should make use of*
>
> Detail 2
>
> Key Words   *problem-solving, working in steps, creativity,*

02-15

| Summarizing | Using your own words, summarize the topic of the lecture, describe how the professor explains the topic, and restate the key points.

Speaking

Now give your spoken response for 60 seconds. You may use the guided response below to assist you.

Using points and examples from the lecture, explain the concept of lateral thinking and how it is used to solve problems in business.

▶ Guided Response

The lecture is about _____, which is _____ when working in logical steps does not _____. Unlike logical thinking, lateral thinking comes from _____ and uses _____. The professor explains that this can be done by _____. He cautions that a business manager should _____, not _____, because anybody could _____. He tells a personal story to _____.

His friend, _____, had a _____ that guests _____. There was no money to _____, so the hotel manager _____. A housekeeper suggested _____.

This solution reduced _____, and it showed how _____ to fix a problem.

| Comparing | Listen to a sample response and compare it with yours.

02-16

(FOCUSING ON PARAPHRASING)

Underline any three sentences in the sample response. Paraphrase each sentence in the space below. Then, practice saying each sentence with natural intonation.

-
-
-

Part **B**

Task 1 Taking a Vacation

Warming Up

Choose a question at random from the list below. Immediately answer the question. Clearly explain your choice and give one detail to support it. Try to speak for at least 20 seconds.

- Where do you enjoy going on vacations?

- What kind of trip is the best?

- Are you the kind of person who prefers to travel alone or with others?

You have a vacation coming up, and you are planning to take a trip. Which of the following would you prefer to do?

- Go camping and spend time away from society

- Stay at a hotel and go sightseeing daily

- Visit a resort and spend most of your time there

Include specific details and reasons in your response.

Brainstorming

Before you plan your response to the prompt, provide a short answer to the critical thinking questions below. Then, fill out the idea web.

| Critical Thinking |

1   What activities do you prefer to do when you take a trip?

2   Which aspects of traveling make it more enjoyable? Which make it less enjoyable?

3   Where did you stay the last time you went on a trip? Why?

| Idea Web |

▶ Choice 1 **Camping**

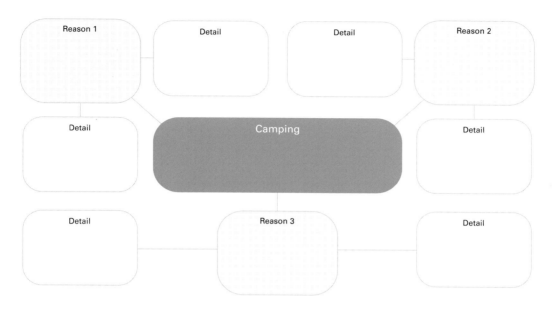

▶ Choice 2 **Hotel**

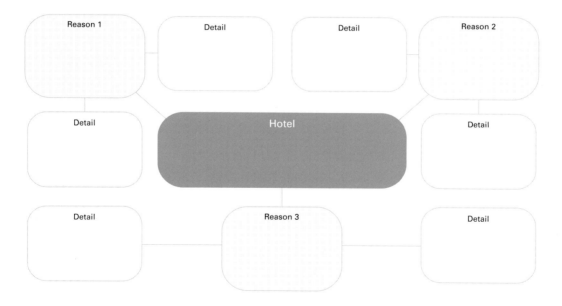

Use your answers to the critical thinking questions and the idea web to organize your response.

> My Choice:
>
> Reason 1:
>
> Reason 2:

Speaking

Now give your spoken response for 45 seconds. You may use the guided response below to assist you.

▶ **Guided Response 1 Go Camping**

I would prefer to _____. One reason I prefer camping is _____.
There is nothing better than _____. I went camping
_____. We spent three days in a forest and had the best trip. In addition, camping
_____. I live in a big city, and _____. There are just
_____. When we went camping, we did not _____. It was so
relaxing to _____ and _____.

▶ **Guided Response 2 Stay at a Hotel**

Of the three choices, I would rather _____. The main reason is that
_____. For example, _____.
That means _____. On my last trip, the hotel my family stayed at
_____. We could _____, which was convenient. Another
reason is that _____. I don't want to _____.
We stayed at _____. We used the money that we saved to
_____. That made our trip much better.

| Comparing | Listen to a sample response and compare it with yours.

Go Camping

02-17

Stay at a
Hotel

02-18

Read the following questions related to the topic. For question 1, use the information provided to make responses. For questions 2 to 6, use your own ideas to make responses.

1 You are taking a trip soon. Which of the following would you prefer to do?
- Fly to your vacation destination
- Drive to your vacation destination

Fly	Drive
- get to destination faster - convenient for destinations far away	- is cheaper than flying - have a way to get around at the destination

2 A holiday is coming soon. Which of the following would you prefer to do?
- Stay home and get some rest
- Meet your friends and socialize with them

Stay Home	Meet Friends

3 Everyone should take a trip to a foreign country at least once in their lives.

Agree	Disagree

4 It is better to travel to nearby places than to visit ones that are far away.

Agree	Disagree

5 Some people like taking one long trip a year. Others prefer to take several short trips a year. Which do you prefer and why?

One Long Trip	Several Short Trips

6 Some people prefer to visit multiple places on a single trip. Others prefer to stay in the same place for their entire trip. Which do you prefer and why?

Visit Multiple Places	Stay in the Same Place

Task 2 Campus Coffee Shop Closing

🔊 Vocabulary Take a few moments to review the vocabulary items that will appear in this task.

---

close [one's] doors *exp.* to go out of business

student council *n.* a campus group that represents student interests

propose *v.* to suggest or recommend an idea

promotional *adj.* in a way that advertises an idea, product, or service

letdown *n.* something that is disappointing

turn [something] around *phr v.* to improve the quality or performance of

dim *adj.* not bright; slightly dark

do the trick *exp.* to accomplish a goal

Reading

Read the following announcement from a campus coffee shop.

Campus Coffee Shop Closing

Following research by the budget and planning staff of City University, the Scholars Café, the campus coffee shop, will close its doors at the end of the semester. The student council first proposed the coffee shop as a place for students to meet with friends and to study in a relaxed environment. Business at the coffee shop has remained slow since its opening despite attempts to advertise, host events, and offer promotional discounts. Because of a lack of student interest, the university will no longer provide funding for the business. Thank you for your understanding.

| **Analyzing** | Answer the following questions. Give brief spoken responses to questions 2-4.

1   What is the purpose of the announcement?
- Ⓐ To introduce a new coffee shop on campus
- Ⓑ To inform students of activities on campus
- Ⓒ To explain why a service will be discontinued
- Ⓓ To advertise recent student council decisions

2   How did the coffee shop try to increase its business?

3   What evidence is given to explain that students are not interested in the coffee shop?

4   **Critical Thinking:** Why might a student be unhappy about this announcement?

Listen to a short conversation related to the reading. Take notes about the man's opinion.

> **Notes**
>
> The man _____ with the decision in the announcement.
>
> Reason 1 *believes the coffee shop could stay open if it*
>
> Reason 2
>
> Key Words and Details *university's position, lighting,*

02-19

| **Summarizing** | In your own words, explain the man's opinion about the announcement.

Give brief spoken responses to the questions based on the announcement and the conversation.

1   Why does the man make suggestions to improve the coffee shop Scholars Café?

2   What reason does the man give for wanting the Scholars Café to stay open?

3   In the man's opinion, why is the Scholars Café not a good place to study?

Now give your spoken response for 60 seconds. You may use the guided response below to assist you.

[?] The man expresses his opinion about the announcement. Explain his opinion and the reasons he gives for holding it.

▶ **Guided Response**

The conversation is about an announcement that _____ .

The student council intended the coffee shop as _____ . However,

students _____ , so _____ . The man thinks that

_____ is unnecessary and that _____ if the coffee shop

_____ . His first idea is that _____ . The current

lighting is _____ , which makes it _____ . The man says the

lighting should _____ , which is _____ . The other idea he has is

_____ . He thinks that more _____ would encourage people to

_____ . Based on these ideas, the man thinks _____ .

| **Comparing** | Listen to a sample response and compare it with yours.

02-20

FOCUSING ON TRANSITIONS

Underline all the transition words and phrases used in the sample response. Write them in the space below and practice saying them with natural intonation.

- _____
- _____
- _____
- _____

Task 3 Education: Active Learning

◉ Vocabulary Take a few moments to review the vocabulary items that will appear in this task.

passive *adj.* receiving action without responding

collaboration *n.* working together

role-play *v.* to do a learning exercise during which students act as characters

medieval *adj.* relating to the period between the 5th and 15th centuries

peasant *n.* a person in the lowest social class

reenact *v.* to perform a historical story, as in a play

no matter which *exp.* shows that all choices are equal

tradeoff *n.* a situation during which a person gives up one thing to gain another

Reading

Read the following passage about active learning.

Active Learning

In a traditional classroom setting, students read material from a textbook and listen to a lecture on the material. This style of learning is known as passive learning. In recent years, educators have become interested in active learning methods. These include several techniques that require student participation. Examples range from basic activities such as class discussions to more complex processes involving group collaborations and presentations. Research shows that active learning results in greater rates of retention as it sometimes doubles or even triples the amount of information students can remember.

| Analyzing | Answer the following questions. Give brief spoken responses to questions 2-4.

1 According to the passage, why are active learning methods being used?

    Ⓐ They are more effective than older learning methods.

    Ⓑ Research shows that students want new learning methods.

    Ⓒ Students do not have enough textbook material to study.

    Ⓓ Basic activities have become boring for students.

2 How does active learning differ from passive learning?

3 What are the benefits of active learning?

4 **Critical Thinking:** How could active learning be used to learn a language?

Listen to a short lecture related to the reading. Take notes on key words and specific information from the lecture.

Notes

02-21

Topic *how active learning*

Detail 1 *personal story about role-playing used to learn*

Detail 2

Key Words *creative approach, medieval Europe,*

| **Summarizing** | In your own words, restate the main idea and the key points of the lecture.

Give brief spoken responses to the questions based on the reading passage and the lecture.

1 Why does the professor begin the lecture by telling a personal story?

2 What information in the reading passage does the lecture clarify?

3 According to the professor, how is active learning a tradeoff?

Now give your spoken response for 60 seconds. You may use the guided response below to assist you.

The professor explains the concept of active learning. Summarize the points made in the lecture and how they relate to the reading.

▶ Guided Response

Active learning is the name given to _____ . They differ from

_____ in which students simply _____ , and they have

been shown to be more effective for _____ . Active learning can be one of various

methods, such as _____ and _____ . The professor

illustrates the concept by _____ . In a _____ class, the

professor decided to _____ . Each student _____ . For

example, some students _____ , another was _____ , and others were

_____ . The students _____ . The professor said that the role-playing

_____ . She also states that the students _____ ,

which demonstrates _____ mentioned in the reading.

| Comparing | Listen to a sample response and compare it with yours.

02-22

(**FOCUSING ON PRONUNCIATION**)

Circle five words in the sample response that you have difficulty pronouncing. Write them in the space below. Practice saying these words in a North American accent.

1 _____   2 _____   3 _____

4 _____   5 _____

Task 4 The Arts: Sculpture

🔊 **Vocabulary** Take a few moments to review the vocabulary items that will appear in this task.

marble *n.* a kind of rock used in architecture and art

chip away *phr v.* to cut small pieces from a larger object

sculpt *v.* to shape clay or rocks into a 3-D form

master *v.* to become an expert

precision *n.* the state of being exact or accurate

carve *v.* to cut a shape into a hard substance

bronze *n.* a metal mixture of copper and tin

cement *n.* a building material that dries rock hard

flexible *adj.* able to be moved or bent easily

pose *n.* a way of positioning the body

Listening

Listen to a lecture on the topic of subtractive sculpture and additive sculpture. Take notes on key words and concepts in the lecture.

> **Notes**
>
> **Topic** *two types of sculpture:*
>
> **Detail 1** *subtractive sculpture = artist starts with a block and*
>
> *most difficult type because*
>
> **Detail 2**
>
> **Key Words** *marble block, total precision,*

02-23

| **Summarizing** | Using your own words, summarize the topic of the lecture, describe how the professor explains the topic, and restate the key points.

Speaking

Now give your spoken response for 60 seconds. You may use the guided response below to assist you.

 Using points and examples from the lecture, explain subtractive sculpture and additive sculpture.

Guided Response

The professor gives a lecture about _____ . The professor starts by explaining

_____ , a technique that was used by _____ . To use this technique, the artist

starts with _____ and _____ . According to the professor, it is

difficult _____ . With just one mistake, _____ . Therefore, most

artists use _____ . These help the artists _____ . The professor

then describes _____ , which differs from _____ in that it is

easier to do. The artist begins with _____ and adds _____ .

Once the artist _____ , the sculpture is finished with _____ .

Most artists _____ because it _____ and

_____ .

| Comparing | Listen to a sample response and compare it with yours.

02-24

⌐ **FOCUSING ON PARAPHRASING** ⌐

Underline any three sentences in the sample response. Paraphrase each sentence in the space below. Then, practice saying each sentence with natural intonation.

-
-
-

Part **B**

Task 1 Preferred Study Environment

Warming Up

Choose a question at random from the list below. Immediately answer the question. Clearly explain your choice and give one detail to support it. Try to speak for at least 20 seconds.

- Do you like to play educational games? Why or why not?

- Would you rather study at home or in a library?

- Do you agree or disagree with this statement: Education at all levels should be funded by the government.

Some people need to study in a quiet environment. Other people like to listen to music when they study. Which do you prefer and why? Include specific details and reasons in your response.

Brainstorming

Before you plan your response to the prompt, provide a short answer to the critical thinking questions below. Then, fill out the idea web.

| Critical Thinking |

1   When you study, does music help your concentration or hurt it?

2   Do other noises disturb you if you are studying in a quiet environment?

3   Why is it important to have a comfortable study environment?

| Idea Web |

▶ Choice 1 Quiet

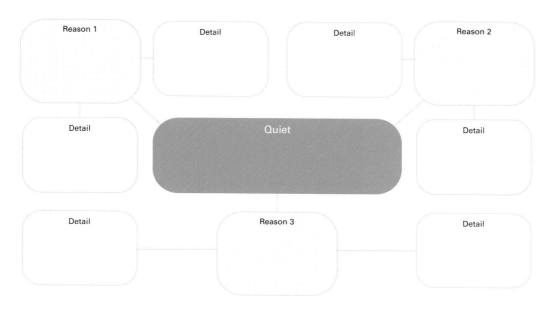

▶ Choice 2 Music

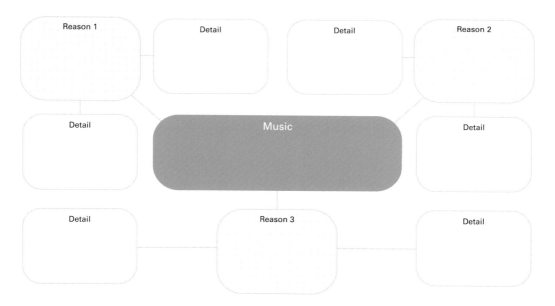

Organizing

Use your answers to the critical thinking questions and the idea web to organize your response.

My Choice:

Reason 1:

Reason 2:

Speaking

Now give your spoken response for 45 seconds. You may use the guided response below to assist you.

▶ **Guided Response 1 Quiet**

When I study, I like _____ . In my experience, listening to music while studying can _____ . My studying is _____ because of my lower level of concentration. Because of this, listening to music while studying _____ , which is something that _____ . I have tried to _____ in the past. I listened to _____ music and even _____ , which my teacher recommended. My test scores _____ . Since that time, I decided _____ . As a result, my grades _____ .

▶ **Guided Response 2 With Music**

I'm the kind of person that likes _____ . When I study, _____ . I listen to music when I study first because it _____ . When the room is quiet, my thoughts _____ . But with music on, I can _____ . My thoughts no longer _____ . Music does more than that. It also helps me _____ . If there is no music, then _____ . So music not only _____ , but it also _____ as well.

| **Comparing** | Listen to a sample response and compare it with yours.

Quiet

With Music

02-25

02-26

70

Read the following questions related to the topic. For question 1, use the information provided to make responses. For questions 2 to 6, use your own ideas to make responses.

1 Some people like to study alone. Other people prefer to study in groups with others. Which do you prefer and why?

Study Alone	Study in Groups
- can study at my own pace	- can ask group members questions
- do not like being distracted by others	- study better when I am with others

2 Some people like to take classes with many students. Others prefer to take classes with few students. Which do you prefer and why?

Classes with Many Students	Classes with Few Students

3 The library is the best place to study.

Agree	Disagree

4 The best teachers are those who let students ask questions during their classes.

Agree	Disagree

5 Students can learn more in classes with discussions than they can in classes during which the teacher only lectures.

Agree	Disagree

6 Online classes are better than in-person classes.

Agree	Disagree

Task 2 Extended Cafeteria Hours

◉ Vocabulary Take a few moments to review the vocabulary items that will appear in this task.

altered *adj.* changed; different

institute *v.* to put into effect

mess *n.* something that is disorganized

starving *adj.* extremely hungry

Reading

Read the following announcement from a club at a university.

Extended Cafeteria Hours

Beginning on Monday, May 3, and continuing until Friday, May 14, the on-campus student cafeteria will extend its operating hours. The regular closing time of 9:00 PM will change to 1:00 AM from Monday through Saturday and to 11:00 PM on Sunday. The altered time schedule will be instituted in order to provide students greater flexibility in their schedules during final exams. Food service will continue until the regular time of 9:00 PM, but sandwiches, fruit, snacks, and beverages will be available until closing time.

| Analyzing | Answer the following questions. Give brief spoken responses to questions 2-4.

1   The purpose of the announcement is to
   Ⓐ encourage students to study at in cafeteria
   Ⓑ propose a change to the cafeteria's hours
   Ⓒ inform students of the additional cafeteria hours
   Ⓓ give students more options for study times

2   How many more hours per week will the cafeteria stay open?

3   What does the announcement state is the purpose of the change?

4   **Critical Thinking:** What effect might this change have on students' study habits?

Listen to a short conversation related to the reading. Take notes about the man's opinion.

> **Notes**
>
> The man feels _____ about the announcement.
>
> Reason 1   *is usually hungry and has to eat junk food after studying; now*
>
> Reason 2
>
> Key Words and Details   *helpful, finals week,*

02-27

| **Summarizing** | In your own words, explain the man's opinion about the announcement.

Synthesizing

Give brief spoken responses to the questions based on the announcement and the conversation.

1   How does the man think the change will affect his health?

2   Why does the man mention that his roommate goes to bed early?

3   According to the woman, what makes the cafeteria a good place to study?

Now give your spoken response for 60 seconds. You may use the guided response below to assist you.

> The man expresses his opinion about the announcement. Explain his opinion and the reasons he gives for holding it.

▸ **Guided Response**

The students are discussing the announcement, which states that _____. The

change is being made because _____. After the change, students will be able

to _____. The man feels _____ because he plans to

_____ during finals week. He says that he will _____ after

he meets with his study groups. This is good because he can _____ instead of

eating _____. Usually, he eats _____. So this will be good for

_____. His other reason is that he can _____ in the cafeteria.

His roommate _____, and the cafeteria is _____, which makes

it a good place _____.

| **Comparing** | Listen to a sample response and compare it with yours.

02-28

⌐ **FOCUSING ON TRANSITIONS** ⌐

Underline all the transition words and phrases used in the sample response. Write them in the space below and practice saying them with natural intonation.

- _____ • _____

- _____ • _____

Task 3 Life Science: Commensalism

🔊 Vocabulary Take a few moments to review the vocabulary items that will appear in this task.

detriment *n.* harm to the health or wellbeing of

exclude *v.* to leave out; to remove from a list of options

parasitism *n.* a relationship in which one organism benefits but causes harm to another

mutualism *n.* a relationship in which both organisms benefit

cattle *n.* a group of cows

classic *adj.* typical; of a well-known type

like shooting fish in a barrel *exp.* easy to do

coral reef *n.* a large, underwater rock-like structure

Reading

Read the following passage about commensalism.

Commensalism

In nature, an organism sometimes lives on or near another organism for its own benefit. In a commensal relationship, the host animal is completely unaffected by the presence of the other organism. It differs from both mutualism, a relationship in which both organisms benefit, and parasitism, a relationship in which the host organism is harmed or somehow disadvantaged. Commensalism can be difficult to prove. Even the smallest benefit or detriment to the host animal excludes the possibility of commensalism.

| **Analyzing** | Answer the following questions. Give brief spoken responses to questions 2-4.

1   The passage describes commensalism as

    Ⓐ different from mutualism but similar to parasitism

    Ⓑ similar to mutualism but different from parasitism

    Ⓒ similar to both mutualism and parasitism

    Ⓓ different from both mutualism and parasitism

2   In a commensal relationship, what does the host animal do?

3   Why is commensalism difficult to prove?

4   **Critical Thinking:** What are two animals you know of that demonstrate commensalism?

Listen to a short lecture related to the reading. Take notes on key words and specific information from the lecture.

Notes

Topic   *examples of*

Detail 1   *egrets stand on cows' backs and*

02-29

Detail 2

Key Words   *cattle fields, hang around,*

| **Summarizing** | In your own words, restate the main idea and the key points of the lecture.

Give brief spoken responses to the questions based on the reading passage and the lecture.

1   According to the passage and the lecture, why is commensalism uncommon?

2   How do egrets demonstrate commensalism?

3   What do barnacles do in order to survive without hurting their host?

Now give your spoken response for 60 seconds. You may use the guided response below to assist you.

The professor explains how cows, egrets, and barnacles demonstrate the concept of commensalism. Explain the examples and how they illustrate commensalism.

▶ Guided Response

The professor speaks about _____ . The first relationship,

_____ , happens when _____ . The cows move around, which

makes _____ . Egrets can then _____ . Cows, on the other

hand, do not _____ , and they are not _____ .

The other relationship is between _____ . Whales are large and broad, so

barnacles _____ . The host animal _____ , so the

barnacles _____ . These two relationships demonstrate that sometimes

_____ . This is different from _____ and can be

hard to prove since _____ .

| Comparing | Listen to a sample response and compare it with yours.

02-30

Circle five words in the sample response that you have difficulty pronouncing. Write them in the space below. Practice saying these words in a North American accent.

1 _____   2 _____   3 _____

4 _____   5 _____

Task 4 Zoology: Animal Desert Adaptations

🔊 Vocabulary Take a few moments to review the vocabulary items that will appear in this task.

precipitation *n.* rain, snow, ice, or hail that falls from the sky

thrive *v.* to prosper; to do very well; to be successful

aquatic *adj.* relating to water

burrow *v.* to dig a hole or passage in the ground

shed *v.* to lose; to get rid of

cocoon *n.* a protective covering made by an animal

dormant *adj.* inactive; being in a state of inactivity

vegetation *n.* plant life

Listening

Listen to a lecture on the topic of animal desert adaptations. Take notes on key words and concepts in the lecture.

Notes

Topic   *two animals that*

Detail 1   *African bullfrog = burrows into the ground in*

02-31

Detail 2

Key Words   *burrows into the ground; sheds its skin;*

| Summarizing | Using your own words, summarize the topic of the lecture, describe how the professor explains the topic, and restate the key points.

Now give your spoken response for 60 seconds. You may use the guided response below to assist you.

Using points and examples from the lecture, explain how the African bullfrog and the desert bighorn sheep have adapted to life in the desert.

▶ Guided Response

The professor talks about _____ and how _____ . She points out that the African bullfrog _____ . It can _____ . The skin then _____ and can _____ . The bullfrog can become dormant for more than a year as it _____ . As for the desert bighorn sheep, it doesn't need to drink water in summer because _____ . It can also use its horns to _____ . Finally, the sheep can _____ . That gives it enough time to _____ .

| Comparing | Listen to a sample response and compare it with yours.

02-32

⌐ **FOCUSING ON PARAPHRASING** ⌐

Underline any three sentences in the sample response. Paraphrase each sentence in the space below. Then, practice saying each sentence with natural intonation.

-
-
-

Part B

Chapter 05

Task 1 Advantages and Disadvantages of Asking Questions

Warming Up

Choose a question at random from the list below. Immediately answer the question. Clearly explain your choice and give one detail to support it. Try to speak for at least 20 seconds.

- When you do not understand something, what do you do?
- Who do you trust when you need to ask someone a question?
- Do you prefer asking your teachers or friends for explanations?

Some people prefer to ask questions to their friends when they do not understand something while others prefer to ask their teachers for help. Talk about the advantages and disadvantages of asking friends [teachers] questions. Use details and examples to explain your answer.

Brainstorming

Before you plan your response to the prompt, provide a short answer to the critical thinking questions below. Then, fill out the idea web.

| Critical Thinking |

1   Who do you feel more comfortable asking questions to?

2   What are some advantages of asking each person?

3   What are some drawbacks to asking each person?

| Idea Web |

▶ **Choice 1 Friends**

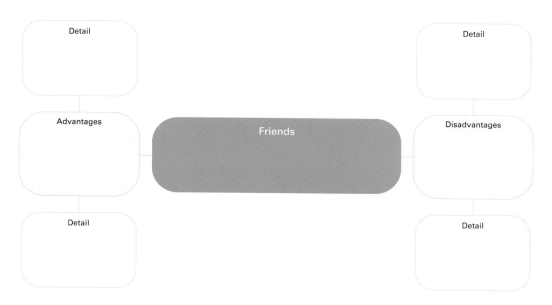

▶ **Choice 2 Teachers**

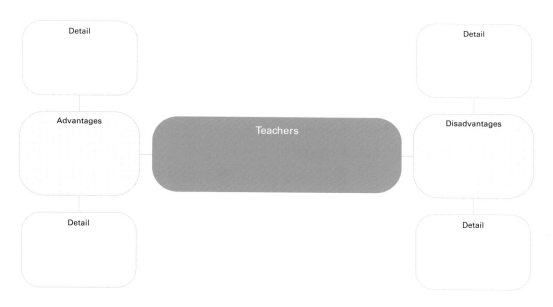

Organizing

Use your answers to the critical thinking questions and the idea web to organize your response.

My Choice:

Advantages:

Disadvantages:

Speaking

Now give your spoken response for 45 seconds. You may use the guided response below to assist you.

⯈ Guided Response 1 Ask Friends

There are both advantages and disadvantages to _____.
As for advantages, friends know _____. I asked my
friend _____ the other day, and _____. I was able
easily to understand it. As for the disadvantages, sometimes _____ or
_____. This is especially true if _____. In addition, a friend
might _____. My friend asked me _____ last week, but I
didn't know the correct answer. She should have _____.

⯈ Guided Response 2 Ask Teachers

I can think of both advantages and disadvantages to _____.
First, one advantage is that _____. This means they should be able
to _____. In addition, teachers _____, so they
_____. On the other hand, there are also disadvantages. For
example, _____. They also might not _____. My science
teacher always _____. Her answers aren't helpful. And some teachers might think
_____. I don't want _____, so I don't always ask question
in class.

| **Comparing** | Listen to a sample response and compare it with yours.

Ask
Friends

Ask
Teachers

02-33   02-34

Read the following questions related to the topic. For question 1, use the information provided to make responses. For questions 2 to 6, use your own ideas to make responses.

1 Some people prefer to take notes in class while others prefer to listen to their teachers lecture. Talk about the advantages and disadvantages of taking notes in class.

Advantages	Disadvantages
- won't forget important information - easier to study for tests later	- cannot write fast → don't write everything down - too busy writing so can't pay attention to lecture

2 Some people prefer to take notes in class while others prefer to listen to their teachers lecture. Talk about the advantages and disadvantages of listening to teachers lecture.

Advantages	Disadvantages

3 Some people prefer to take classes with fun instructors while others prefer to take classes with serious instructors. Talk about the advantages and disadvantages of taking classes with fun instructors.

Advantages	Disadvantages

4 Some people prefer to take classes with fun instructors while others prefer to take classes with more serious instructors. Talk about the advantages and disadvantages of taking classes with serious instructors.

Advantages	Disadvantages

5 Some people prefer to do all of their homework at school while others prefer to do their school assignments at home. Talk about the advantages and disadvantages of doing homework at school.

Advantages	Disadvantages

6 Some people prefer to do all of their homework at school while others prefer to do their school assignments at home. Talk about the advantages and disadvantages of doing school assignments at home.

Advantages	Disadvantages

Task 2 New Literature Major Requirements

🔊 **Vocabulary** Take a few moments to review the vocabulary items that will appear in this task.

thesis *n.* a lengthy essay used to prove academic achievement

conduct *v.* to carry out; to perform

committee *n.* a group that makes decisions for an organization

premise *n.* the basis for an argument

lit *n.* an abbreviation for "literature"

is no joke *exp.* shows that something is difficult

undergraduate *adj.* relating to the basic four-year course at a university

have [it] all worked out *exp.* to have answers for or a plan to solve a challenge

Reading

Read the following announcement from the head of the Department of Literature.

New Requirements for Literature Majors

Effective this semester, all Literature majors now have an additional requirement for graduation. In order to receive a diploma in Literature, students are required to write a senior thesis. Upon beginning their senior year, students will be assigned an advisor who will assist in choosing an appropriate topic, conducting research, and writing. The thesis will be due no later than two weeks prior to the end of the semester. After review by a committee, students must defend the arguments and the premises within their thesis. Students who fail to pass the committee's examination will not be eligible for graduation.

| Analyzing | Answer the following questions. Give brief spoken responses to questions 2-4.

1 The purpose of the announcement is to

   Ⓐ warn students not to major in Literature

   Ⓑ help Literature majors choose an advisor

   Ⓒ create a new major in the Literature Department

   Ⓓ advise Literature majors of a new policy

2 How do students create their senior thesis?

3 What happens to the senior thesis after a student writes it?

4 **Critical Thinking:** How might the new requirement benefit Literature majors?

Listen to a short conversation related to the reading. Take notes about the man's opinion.

Notes

The man feels _____ about the announcement.

Reason 1   *can help him identify his weaknesses by*

Reason 2

Key Words and Details   *professional writer, develop my skills,*

02-35

| Summarizing | In your own words, explain the man's opinion about the announcement.

Synthesizing

Give brief spoken responses to the questions based on the announcement and the conversation.

1   How will the information in the announcement affect the man?

2   In what ways does the man think he will benefit as a result of the change?

3   What does the man think about student-teacher interaction?

Now give your spoken response for 60 seconds. You may use the guided response below to assist you.

The man expresses his opinion about the announcement. Explain his opinion and the reasons he gives for holding it.

▶ **Guided Response**

The announcement states that _____ . After writing it,

the thesis must be _____ . Literature students cannot graduate unless

_____ . The man reacts _____ to the announcement. He thinks

that, overall, it will _____ . The first reason he gives for his opinion is

_____ . He wants to become a professional writer, and the thesis will

help him _____ . In that way, he can improve _____ .

The other reason he gives is that _____ . He believes this is true because

_____ . As a result, he will learn _____ .

│ **Comparing** │ Listen to a sample response and compare it with yours.

02-36

⌐ **FOCUSING ON TRANSITIONS** ┐

Underline all the transition words and phrases used in the sample response. Write them in the space below and practice saying them with natural intonation.

· _____   · _____

· _____   · _____

Task 3 Human Biology: The Immune System

Vocabulary Take a few moments to review the vocabulary items that will appear in this task.

infectious *adj.* able to be spread from one person to another

alert *v.* to warn of approaching danger or action

rid *v.* to remove from a location or system

microorganism *n.* an organism so small that it cannot be seen by the naked eye

swell up *phr v.* to expand abnormally

concentrate *v.* to meet in a common center

kick out *phr v.* to force to leave

expel *v.* to force or drive away

Reading

Read the following passage about the immune system.

The Immune System

Inside the human body exists a network of cells, tissues, and organs that work together to defend the body against invading organisms and infectious bacteria. This network is called the immune system, and it is responsible for keeping people healthy. Without the immune system, humans would not have survived very long as a species. The immune system alerts people when there is a problem and if possible, takes direct action to rid the invading cells from people's bodies.

| Analyzing | Answer the following questions. Give brief spoken responses to questions 2-4.

1 What is the passage mainly about?
- Ⓐ How the immune system fights against disease
- Ⓑ The human body's method of protecting itself
- Ⓒ What to do if a person is attacked by an invading organism
- Ⓓ Alert messages sent to the body by bacteria

2 According to the passage, what is the importance of the immune system?

3 How does the immune system perform its function?

4 **Critical Thinking:** How do you think the immune system alerts us of problems?

Listen to a short lecture related to the reading. Take notes on key words and specific information from the lecture.

Notes

Topic   *ways the immune system*

Detail 1   *white blood cells are produced when*

02-37

Detail 2

Key Words   *parasites, white blood cells, invading bacteria,*

| **Summarizing** | In your own words, restate the main idea and the key points of the lecture.

Give brief spoken responses to the questions based on the reading passage and the lecture.

1   What additional information does the professor provide about the immune system?

2   Which examples does the professor use to explain the immune system's function?

3   How does the lecture explain the alerts mentioned in the reading passage?

Now give your spoken response for 60 seconds. You may use the guided response below to assist you.

The professor gives examples of the immune system. Explain the examples and how they illustrate the ways that the immune system protects the body from infection.

Guided Response

The professor begins with a brief introduction to _____ . As explained in the reading,

the immune system is _____ that protect the body from _____ .

The professor mentions that bacteria are _____ , so the body wants to _____ . She clarifies

the topic by giving _____ . The first example, _____ ,

demonstrates how the body _____ . The immune system produces

_____ , which _____ . We can observe this happening when

_____ . The second example, _____ , shows that the immune system may

attempt to _____ . When the immune system _____ , it may

_____ , which will hopefully _____ .

| Comparing | Listen to a sample response and compare it with yours.

02-38

FOCUSING ON PRONUNCIATION

Circle five words in the sample response that you have difficulty pronouncing. Write them in the space below. Practice saying these words in a North American accent.

1 _____   2 _____   3 _____

4 _____   5 _____

Task 4 Animal Science: Cooperative Hunting

Q Vocabulary Take a few moments to review the vocabulary items that will appear in this task.

never-ending *adj.* continuing without any sign of stopping

strategy *n.* a plan of action

alongside *adv.* together with; in cooperation with

observe *v.* to watch carefully

roam *v.* to move about in no particular direction

advantageous *adj.* providing some benefits or advantages

lone *adj.* by oneself; with no others

complementary *adj.* making something perfect or whole

Listening

Listen to a lecture on the topic of coopperative hunting techniques. Take notes on key words and concepts in the lecture.

Notes

Topic *cooperative hunting =*

Detail 1 *pack hunting = animals of the same species hunting together*

ex: wild dogs

Detail 2

02-39

Key Words *technique, at least nine dogs, group of prey,*

| **Summarizing** | Using your own words, summarize the topic of the lecture, describe how the professor explains the topic, and restate the key points.

Speaking

Now give your spoken response for 60 seconds. You may use the guided response below to assist you.

Using points and examples from the lecture, explain cooperative hunting and how it can be beneficial.

▶ **Guided Response**

The professor is explaining _____. Put simply, this is when

_____. There are two basic types of _____. The first is

_____. The professor explains it by _____. Whenever

wild dogs _____, they _____. This provides them with

benefits because _____. So cooperative hunting improves

_____. The second type is _____. This is when two animals

of _____. The professor discusses _____ to demonstrate this

kind of hunting. The grouper fish _____. Other times, the moray eel

_____. Both animals benefit because _____.

| **Comparing** | Listen to a sample response and compare it with yours.

02-40

⌐ **FOCUSING ON PARAPHRASING** ⌐

Underline any three sentences in the sample response. Paraphrase each sentence in the space below. Then, practice saying each sentence with natural intonation.

-
-
-

Part **B**

Task 1 University: Hometown vs. Out of Town

Warming Up

Choose a question at random from the list below. Immediately answer the question. Clearly explain your choice and give one detail to support it. Try to speak for at least 20 seconds.

- Is education necessary for a successful career?

- Do you enjoy traveling?

- Agree or disagree: Book knowledge is more valuable than life experience.

Would you prefer to go to a university in your hometown or in another city? Include specific details and reasons in your response.

Brainstorming

Before you plan your response to the prompt, provide a short answer to the critical thinking questions below. Then, fill out the idea web.

| Critical Thinking |

1   What are the challenges of moving to a new city?

2   What are the benefits of staying in your hometown?

3   How would each option better allow you to achieve your goals in university?

| Idea Web |

▶ Choice 1 Hometown

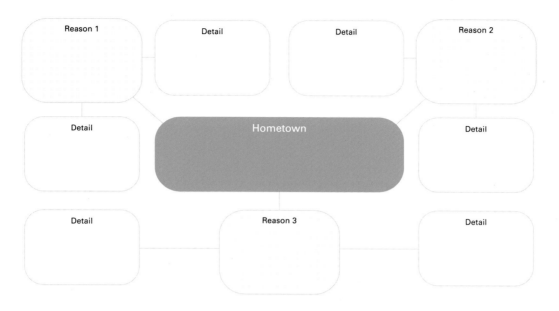

▶ Choice 2 Another City

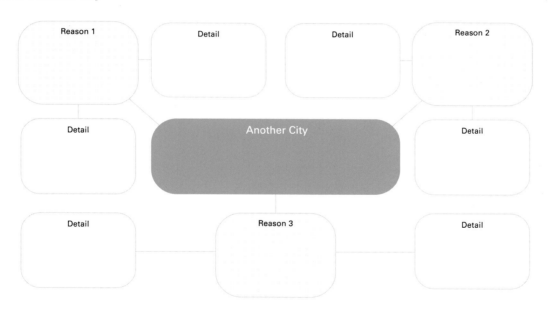

Organizing

Use your answers to the critical thinking questions and the idea web to organize your response.

My Choice:

Reason 1:

Reason 2:

Speaking

Now give your spoken response for 45 seconds. You may use the guided response below to assist you.

▶ Guided Response 1 Hometown

When I go to university, I would like to _____ . While moving away may be

adventurous, I think staying home _____ . As a practical person, staying

in my hometown would allow me to _____ . Because I would not have to

_____ , I would have more _____ . For example, I could

_____ . In addition to that, moving away would _____ . That

stress does not _____ . I can _____ and not worry about

_____ . That way, I could focus more on _____ .

▶ Guided Response 2 Another City

I believe that _____ would _____ . Therefore, I would not stay

_____ . I know someone who stayed _____ .

I noticed that she _____ . This leads me to think that moving away

_____ . This would help me to grow as a person because

_____ . Besides that, moving away would give me the opportunity

to _____ . One of my goals in university will be _____ . If I stay

at home, I cannot _____ because _____ .

| Comparing | Listen to a sample response and compare it with yours.

Hometown

Another
City

02-41

02-42

Read the following questions related to the topic. For question 1, use the information provided to make responses. For questions 2 to 6, use your own ideas to make responses.

1 Would you prefer to major in a subject that you already know a lot about or one which you know little about?

Know a Lot About	Know Little About
- can help me get better grades - can understand the material more easily	- have an opportunity to learn more - want to major in an interesting topic even if I know nothing about it

2 Would you prefer to live in a dormitory at a university or to live at your home while you attend school?

Live in a Dormitory	Live at Home

3 Would you prefer to take out a loan to pay your university tuition or to get a part-time job during the semester to pay for school?

Take Out a Loan	Get a Part-Time Job

4 The biggest cities in my country have the best universities.

Agree	Disagree

5 It is better to attend a small university than one with many students.

Agree	Disagree

6 All university students should be required to study at least one foreign language.

Agree	Disagree

Task 2 Healthy Food Options

Q Vocabulary Take a few moments to review the vocabulary items that will appear in this task.

conscious *adj.* concerned about; actively aware of

alarmed *adj.* surprised and upset

growl *v.* to make a low, steady sound, especially like one made by angry dogs

break *n.* a period of rest between classes or work

diet *n.* the food that one eats

hardly *adv.* almost not; barely

Reading

Read the following letter to the student newspaper.

Campus Stores Needs Healthy Options

As a health-conscious student, I am alarmed by the food options provided at the convenience stores on campus. Sometimes I stop in for a quick snack between classes hoping to find something to ease my growling stomach. Unfortunately, the only options are candy bars, salty potato chips, greasy hotdogs, and other equally unhealthy choices. This selection of junk food is unacceptable. It would be nice to see some fresh fruit, salads, and other healthy products for students to choose from.

Beverly DeLauro
Junior

| **Analyzing** | Answer the following questions. Give brief spoken responses to questions 2-4.

1   The writer of the letter hopes to
   Ⓐ have healthy food on campus
   Ⓑ stop eating junk food
   Ⓒ begin a weight-loss program
   Ⓓ eat a snack between classes

2   How does the writer describe herself?

3   Why does the writer mention fresh fruit and salads?

4   **Critical Thinking:** Why might students object to the letter writer's requests?

Listen to a short conversation related to the reading. Take notes about the woman's opinion.

> ### Notes
>
> The woman _____ with the letter.
>
> Reason 1   *does not have much time between classes and wants to*
>
> Reason 2
>
> Key Words and Details   *junk food, busy schedule, one-hour break,*

02-43

| Summarizing | In your own words, explain the woman's opinion about the letter.

Synthesizing

Give brief spoken responses to the questions based on the letter and the conversation.

1   How does the woman personalize the ideas in the letter?

2   Why can the woman not eat healthy meals at the cafeteria?

3   What does the woman think part of the role of a university is?

Now give your spoken response for 60 seconds. You may use the guided response below to assist you.

The woman expresses her opinion about the letter. Explain her opinion and the reasons she gives for holding it.

▶ Guided Response

The woman expresses her opinion about _____. In the letter, a student says _____. The current options on campus are _____.
The woman _____ with this for two reasons. First, she says that _____. She explains that her schedule _____.
Therefore, she does not have time _____. Second, she explains that a university _____. The food options available now promote _____, which the woman thinks _____. By selling healthier options, _____. Therefore, she thinks the letter _____.

| **Comparing** | Listen to a sample response and compare it with yours.

02-44

FOCUSING ON TRANSITIONS

Underline all the transition words and phrases used in the sample response. Write them in the space below and practice saying them with natural intonation.

- _____
- _____

- _____
- _____

Task 3 Zoology: Pack Behavior

🔊 **Vocabulary** Take a few moments to review the vocabulary items that will appear in this task.

migrate *v.* to move from one place to another, often for food or mating

social system *n.* a set of cultural and structural elements in a group

alpha male *n.* the most dominant male in a group

mutual *adj.* shared in common

challenge *v.* to threaten; to provoke one into a fight

territory *n.* the land claimed by an animal or group of animals

behavior *n.* how a person or animal acts

Reading

Read the following passage about pack behavior.

Pack Behavior

Some animals, particularly wild dogs and wolves, live together in groups. These groups, which may include fifteen or more animals, are called packs. Animals in packs live, migrate, hunt, and eat together. The pack provides a social system for the animals. The leader is the alpha male or female. Higher-ranking animals are betas while the lowest animal is the omega. The social standing of each animal determines activities such as when the animal can eat after a kill. There are numerous advantages to living in a pack, including mutual safety for the animals.

| **Analyzing** | Answer the following questions. Give brief spoken responses to questions 2-4.

1 The passage defines a pack as

    Ⓐ a prey animal that avoids predators

    Ⓑ a group of alpha males and females

    Ⓒ an animal that lives by itself

    Ⓓ a group of animals that lives together

2 What do animals in packs do together?

3 What are some different animals in a pack called?

4 **Critical Thinking:** What are some possible advantages of animals living together in a pack?

Listen to a short lecture related to the reading. Take notes on key words and specific information from the lecture.

Notes

Topic   *how packs*

Detail 1   *can hunt*

   can hunt large animals;

Detail 2

Key Words   *hunt much better; hunt larger animals;*

02-45

| **Summarizing** | In your own words, restate the main idea and the key points of the lecture.

Synthesizing

Give brief spoken responses to the questions based on the reading passage and the lecture.

1 How does the professor's lecture show pack behavior?

2 What disadvantages does the professor discuss about lone wolves?

3 Based on the reading and the lecture, how can wolves benefit from pack behavior?

Now give your spoken response for 60 seconds. You may use the guided response below to assist you.

The professor talks about wolves. Explain how their actions are related to pack behavior.

▶ **Guided Response**

The professor lectures to the students _____. He points out that wolves often

_____. There are two main benefits to _____. First, lone wolves

_____. However, wolves in packs _____.

Those kills can give wolves _____. Second, wolves can be _____.

Lone wolves may _____, but few animals will _____.

The actions of wolves are related to _____. Pack behavior describes

_____. Each animal in a pack, including _____

_____, has its behavior determined _____.

| Comparing | Listen to a sample response and compare it with yours.

02-46

⌐ **FOCUSING ON PRONUNCIATION** ⌐

Circle five words in the sample response that you have difficulty pronouncing. Write them in the space below.
Practice saying these words in a North American accent.

1 _____   2 _____   3 _____

4 _____   5 _____

Task 4 Business: Targeted Marketing

● Vocabulary Take a few moments to review the vocabulary items that will appear in this task.

target *v.* to aim at or focus on

segment *n.* one part of a whole

identify *v.* to learn the identity of

cologne *n.* a scented spray used by men

overwhelmingly *adv.* extremely in effect or strength

cruise trip *n.* a holiday vacation on a luxury ship

billboard *n.* a large roadside sign used for advertising

all walks of life *exp.* various social groups

Listening

Listen to a lecture on the topic of targeted marketing. Take notes on key words and concepts in the lecture.

Notes

Topic *examples of when to use*

Detail 1 *marketing that targets specific groups of*

   ex: women's magazine ads, such as

Detail 2

Key Words *specific segments, direct advertising, children's toys,*

02-47

| **Summarizing** | Using your own words, summarize the topic of the lecture, describe how the professor explains the topic, and restate the key points.

Now give your spoken response for 60 seconds. You may use the guided response below to assist you.

Using points and examples from the lecture, explain targeted marketing.

▶ Guided Response

The topic of the lecture is _____ . The professor briefly defines this as

_____ . To illustrate the concept, the professor first gives examples of

_____ . He explains that in _____ , you'll find advertisements for

things like _____ . In _____ ,

you'll see advertisements for _____ but not for paper towels. The reason is that

_____ , so the advertising is _____ .

The last part of the lecture talks about _____ . For some products, targeted

marketing _____ . This is illustrated with the example of

_____ . Since all kinds of people _____ , you should advertise in

_____ .

| Comparing | Listen to a sample response and compare it with yours.

02-48

FOCUSING ON PARAPHRASING

Underline any three sentences in the sample response. Paraphrase each sentence in the space below. Then, practice saying each sentence with natural intonation.

-
-
-

Part **B**

Task 1 Overpaid Entertainers

Warming Up

Choose a question at random from the list below. Immediately answer the question. Clearly explain your choice and give one detail to support it. Try to speak for at least 20 seconds.

- Are you influenced by celebrities?

- Would you prefer to be a pop star or a successful scientist?

- Should a doctor earn more money than a police officer?

Some people believe that entertainers, such as pop singers and professional athletes, are overpaid. Do you agree or disagree with that opinion? Include specific details and reasons in your response.

Brainstorming

Before you plan your response to the prompt, provide a short answer to the critical thinking questions below. Then, fill out the idea web.

| Critical Thinking |

1   Why are entertainers often paid large salaries?

2   How do the salaries of other professions compare to the salaries of entertainers?

3   Who deserves to make the highest salaries in society? The lowest?

| Idea Web |

▶ Choice 1 Agree

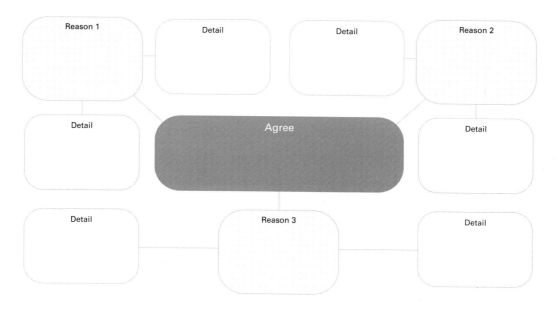

▶ Choice 2 Disagree

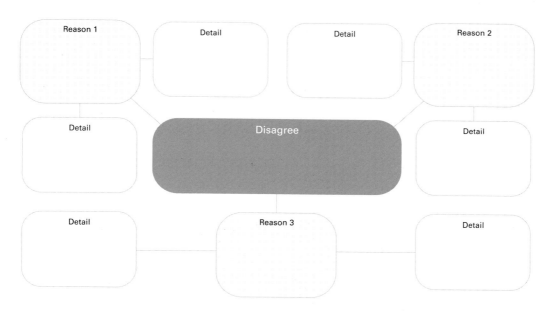

Organizing

Use your answers to the critical thinking questions and the idea web to organize your response.

> **My Choice:**
>
> **Reason 1:**
>
> **Reason 2:**

Speaking

Now give your spoken response for 45 seconds. You may use the guided response below to assist you.

▶ **Guided Response 1 Agree**

It is clear that entertainers _____. They earn far more _____.

Their salaries are too high. I believe that a salary should be determined by _____.

Entertainers do not _____, so they should not _____.

Other professions, such as _____ more money. Another reason is

that _____. When I see entertainers, I notice that _____. If

entertainers did not earn such high salaries, _____. I think everyone

would agree that _____.

▶ **Guided Response 2 Disagree**

I am of the belief that _____. I think that entertainers work _____.

Many people think it is a _____ lifestyle, but _____.

They must deal with _____. This makes their jobs difficult, so

_____. I would also argue that entertainers are _____.

They provide society with _____. This is valuable to society because

_____. Because of their importance to society,

_____. That's why I think _____.

| **Comparing** | Listen to a sample response and compare it with yours.

Agree

02-49

Disagree

02-50

Related Topics

Read the following questions related to the topic. For question 1, use the information provided to make responses. For questions 2 to 6, use your own ideas to make responses.

1 Teachers are not paid enough.

Agree	Disagree
- have important jobs - good ones quit to make more money at other jobs	- do not work during vacations → shouldn't get paid more - many lazy teachers → don't deserve higher salaries

2 Companies that do not pay their employees high salaries should provide them with more benefits.

Agree	Disagree

3 People today spend too much time talking about the personal lives of celebrities.

Agree	Disagree

4 People in the entertainment industry provide valuable services to society.

Agree	Disagree

5 Movies that were made several decades ago are more entertaining than movies made in the present day.

Agree	Disagree

6 Performers in movies in the past were more talented than performers in the present day.

Agree	Disagree

Task 2 Boat Rentals

🔊 **Vocabulary** Take a few moments to review the vocabulary items that will appear in this task.

rent *v.* to charge money to let a person use something for a certain amount of time

minimum *adj.* being the least possible

fee *n.* money a person pays for a service

pastime *n.* a free-time activity; something a person does that makes time pass pleasantly

mixed feelings *phr n.* a partly positive and partly negative reaction to something

habit *n.* a regular activity a person does

recover *v.* to get back something that was spent or lost

invest *v.* to spend money on something in the hope of making more money in the future

Reading

Read the following letter to a student newspaper.

Boat Rentals Too Expensive

I was extremely pleased to learn that the school is renting boats to students who want to sail on Bear Lake. However, my happiness turned to disappointment when I arrived at the lake. I learned that it costs 10 dollars an hour to rent a boat. There is also a two-hour minimum rental fee. That price is simply outrageous. The school needs to understand that most students cannot afford to pay that kind of money. It needs to lower the price immediately. Then, more students will be able to enjoy a fun and relaxing pastime.

Christine Walker
Sophomore

| Analyzing | Answer the following questions. Give brief spoken responses to questions 2-4.

1 The purpose of this letter is to
   Ⓐ thank the school for renting boats
   Ⓑ argue that not enough students are renting boats
   Ⓒ describe an experience while sailing on a boat
   Ⓓ explain why some students have to rent a boat

2 How does the writer support her opinion?

3 What is the main argument presented in the letter?

4 **Critical Thinking:** How could lowering the price of boat rentals affect students?

Listen to a short conversation related to the reading. Take notes about the man's opinion.

Notes

02-51

The man has _____ about the letter.

Reason 1   *not possible for many students to*

Reason 2

Key Words and Details   *mixed feelings; could afford to do it once or twice;*

| **Summarizing** | In your own words, explain the man's opinion about the letter.

Synthesizing

Give a brief spoken response to the questions based on the letter and the conversation.

1   How does the man say that he feels about the information in the letter?

2   In what way does the man agree with the writer of the letter?

3   How does the man disagree with the writer of the letter?

Now give your spoken response for 60 seconds. You may use the guided response below to assist you.

The man expresses his opinion about the letter. Explain his opinion and the reasons he gives for holding it.

▶ Guided Response

The man and the woman are talking about _____. The man states that

_____ about the remarks made by the writer of the letter. First of all, he comments that

he agrees that _____. He points out that _____.

About himself, he notes that he _____ but _____. However,

the man also _____. He says that the school _____ and

_____. Because the school has to _____, he thinks that

_____.

| **Comparing** | Listen to a sample response and compare it with yours.

02-52

Underline all the transition words and phrases used in the sample response. Write them in the space below and practice saying them with natural intonation.

- _____   • _____

- _____   • _____

Task 3 Psychology: Sensory Memory

🎧 **Vocabulary** Take a few moments to review the vocabulary items that will appear in this task.

distinguish *v.* to separate as different from something else

momentarily *adv.* for a brief time

subconscious *adj.* unnoticed by the active part of the mind

landmark *adj.* highly important or significant

grid *n.* a pattern of squares made by crossing lines

flash *v.* to occur suddenly and briefly

Reading

Read the following passage about sensory memory.

Sensory Memory

The two most common types of memory known to humans are short-term and long-term memory. In fact, there is a third type of memory known as sensory memory. The name was given to distinguish this type of memory from short-term memory since its duration is much shorter. Studies have shown that the human brain stores visual information without a person even being aware of it happening. While short-term memories may last ten to fifteen seconds, sensory memories last, at most, only one or two seconds.

| Analyzing | Answer the following questions. Give brief spoken responses to questions 2-4.

1 Sensory memory can best be described as
   Ⓐ an automatic and short-lived memory
   Ⓑ the ability to remember for a lifetime
   Ⓒ a problem with a person's memory
   Ⓓ similar to short-term memory

2 How do sensory memories differ from other common types of memory?

3 According to the passage, how are sensory memories formed?

4 **Critical Thinking:** What kinds of things would sensory memory remember?

Listen to a short lecture related to the reading. Take notes on key words and specific information from the lecture.

> **Notes**
>
> **Topic**   *a kind of memory that*
>
> **Detail 1**   *happens subconsciously: if you do not think about the memories, then*
>
> **Detail 2**
>
> **Key Words**   *subconscious level, senses, half a second,*

02-53

| **Summarizing** | In your own words, restate the main idea and the key points of the lecture.

Give a brief spoken response to the questions based on the reading passage and the lecture.

1   What are the two defining qualities of sensory memory?

2   How did the study measure the duration of sensory memories?

3   Why does the professor compare sensory memories to photographs?

Now give your spoken response for 60 seconds. You may use the guided response below to assist you.

The professor explains a study that was done on memory. Explain the study and how it illustrates the concept of sensory memory.

Guided Response

Sensory memory is a kind of memory that _____ . It happens in the _____ , and sometimes we don't _____ . These memories do not _____ . According to the reading, they last _____ .
The professor further explains this idea by _____ . In the study, participants saw _____ . They _____ , and then they were asked to _____ . The experiment showed that participants usually could _____ , or they could _____ . Either way, they typically only _____ . This showed that _____ . If we think quickly, we can _____ . That is called _____ .

| Comparing | Listen to a sample response and compare it with yours.

02-54

FOCUSING ON PRONUNCIATION

Circle five words in the sample response that you have difficulty pronouncing. Write them in the space below. Practice saying these words in a North American accent.

1 _____   2 _____   3 _____

4 _____   5 _____

Task 4 History: Sun Tzu

🅠 Vocabulary   Take a few moments to review the vocabulary items that will appear in this task.

advisor *n.* an expert who gives advice

victorious *adj.* having won a battle or contest

general *n.* a high-ranking leader in a military force

brutal *adj.* showing no kindness or mercy

agriculture *n.* the act of growing food for humans to eat

soldier *n.* a person who serves in an army

Listening

Listen to a lecture about a historical figure. Take notes on key words and concepts in the lecture.

> **Notes**
>
> **Topic**   *Chinese military advisor Sun Tzu influenced*
>
> **Detail 1**   *taught generals to take advantage of the enemy's*
>
>   *China's wars changed from more traditional to*
>
> **Detail 2**
>
> **Key Words**   *military strategy, ruling lord, strategies,*

02-55

| Summarizing | Using your own words, summarize the topic of the lecture, describe how the professor explains the topic, and restate the key points.

Now give your spoken response for 60 seconds. You may use the guided response below to assist you.

Using points and examples from the lecture, explain how the teachings of Sun Tzu influenced military strategy in historical and modern times.

▶ Guided Response

The professor is describing a historical figure, _____, who was _____. Sun Tzu wrote about _____, and his teachings became popular. Using examples from _____, the professor shows _____. In ancient China, fighting was _____. He said that you should _____. Soon after people began studying his strategies, Chinese wars _____. The rulers concentrated on _____. The professor explains that _____ were an influence on Napoleon as well. Napoleon studied Sun Tzu and had success by _____. However, he did not _____. His soldiers _____ because _____. This ignored Sun Tzu's teachings to _____.

| Comparing | Listen to a sample response and compare it with yours.

02-56

FOCUSING ON PARAPHRASING

Underline any three sentences in the sample response. Paraphrase each sentence in the space below. Then, practice saying each sentence with natural intonation.

-
-
-

Part **B**

Task 1 Experienced Teacher vs. New Teacher

Warming Up

Choose a question at random from the list below. Immediately answer the question. Clearly explain your choice and give one detail to support it. Try to speak for at least 20 seconds.

- Do you enjoy bike riding? Why or why not?

- Would you rather play computer games or board games?

- Are educational games a good way to learn?

Would you prefer to have an experienced teacher who is unenthusiastic or a new teacher with lots of energy? Include specific details and reasons in your response.

Brainstorming

Before you plan your response to the prompt, provide a short answer to the critical thinking questions below. Then, fill out the idea web.

| Critical Thinking |

1   How can your emotional state affect your learning?

2   Is a teacher's own knowledge necessary in addition to a course textbook?

3   Do you think teaching is a learned ability or a natural talent?

| Idea Web |

Choice 1 **Experienced Teacher**

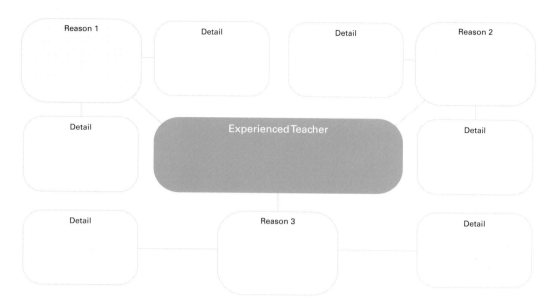

Choice 2 **New Teacher**

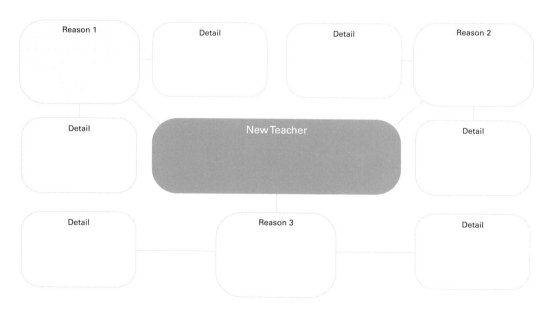

Use your answers to the critical thinking questions and the idea web to organize your response.

My Choice:

Reason 1:

Reason 2:

Now give your spoken response for 45 seconds. You may use the guided response below to assist you.

▶ **Guided Response 1 Experienced Teacher**

Given this choice, I would prefer _____ . Even though a teacher

may be boring, he or she _____ . This is more useful to me as a student because

_____ . For example, one of my teachers _____ . He is not

very fun, but he _____ . Because of this, the students _____ .

Another reason is that an experienced teacher knows _____ . This means

that the teacher can _____ . In a nutshell, I think that an experienced teacher

_____ and _____ .

▶ **Guided Response 2 New Teacher**

As a student, I always prefer a teacher who _____ . Even though the

teacher is new, he or she can _____ . There are a couple of reasons why

_____ . The main reason is that an enthusiastic teacher _____ .

This is very important because _____ . So the teacher's enthusiasm

will automatically improve the _____ . In addition, a new teacher is more likely to

_____ . I find this useful because _____ . In sum, I think a

new, enthusiastic teacher _____ .

| Comparing | Listen to a sample response and compare it with yours.

Experienced   New Teacher
Teacher

02-57   02-58

Related Topics

Read the following questions related to the topic. For question 1, use the information provided to make responses. For questions 2 to 6, use your own ideas to make responses.

1   Would you prefer to take an art class or a science class?

Art Class	Science Class
- show my creative side - want to learn to paint	- can learn important knowledge - enjoy learning about the world and how it works

2   Would you prefer to take a class after school or take part in an extracurricular activity after school?

Take a Class	Take Part in an Extracurricular Activity

3   Would you prefer to be a member of the school band or to belong to an academic club?

School Band	Academic Club

4   Students take too many classes at school these days.

Agree	Disagree

5   Students would be better off if they had the same teacher for all of their classes.

Agree	Disagree

6   The best school are those which encourage their students to play sports or do extracurricular activities.

Agree	Disagree

Task 2 Eating in Class

🎧 **Vocabulary** Take a few moments to review the vocabulary items that will appear in this task.

across the board *exp.* including all items or members of a group

enhance *v.* to change in order to make better

I'm not following you *exp.* an that shows someone does not understand

distraction *n.* something that takes away one's attention

Reading

Read the following announcement about a policy change.

Eating in Class

The student council is pleased to announce that the campus-wide policy against having food in class will no longer apply across the board. Instead, professors will be given the option of allowing students to bring food to class. After a great amount of discussion in the student council, it was concluded that students concentrate better on full stomachs, so having a snack during a lecture may increase classroom participation and enhance the overall learning experience. In addition, the new policy will allow professors the option of having an end-of-semester party with their classes.

| **Analyzing** | Answer the following questions. Give brief spoken responses to questions 2-4.

1 The purpose of the announcement is to
   Ⓐ encourage students to eat in class
   Ⓑ advise against eating during lectures
   Ⓒ explain how a campus rule has changed
   Ⓓ inform students of a new policy

2 How was the decision made?

3 What was the purpose of the decision?

4 **Critical Thinking:** What will be some effects of the decision?

Listen to a short conversation related to the reading. Take notes about the man's opinion.

Notes

The man _____ about the announcement.

Reason 1 *other students eating in class can be a distraction because of*

02-59

Reason 2

Key Words and Details *concentrate, food containers, chew food,*

Summarizing In your own words, explain the man's opinion about the announcement.

Synthesizing

Give brief spoken responses to the questions based on the announcement and the conversation.

1   Why does the man disagree that the decision will increase students' concentration?

2   How does the man expect that the announced decision will affect him?

3   What is the man's opinion about having end-of-semester parties?

Now give your spoken response for 60 seconds. You may use the guided response below to assist you.

The man expresses his opinion about the announcement. Explain his opinion and the reasons he gives for holding it.

▶ **Guided Response**

The man is explaining why _____ , which declares that _____ .
The announcement states that _____ so that they can
_____ and _____ . The man _____ this
rule change. The first reason the man _____ is that he thinks
_____ . He says that _____ . This would
_____ . Furthermore, he states that _____ .
He feels that _____ . Instead of having a party, he would rather
_____ .

| **Comparing** | Listen to a sample response and compare it with yours.

02-60

FOCUSING ON TRANSITIONS

Underline all the transition words and phrases used in the sample response. Write them in the space below and practice saying them with natural intonation.

- _____   • _____

- _____   • _____

Task 3 Business: Aggressive Marketing

Ⓥ Vocabulary Take a few moments to review the vocabulary items that will appear in this task.

dozens *n*. a large, unspecific number

stand out *phr v*. to be noticed amongst a large group

tactic *n*. a plan for achieving a goal

out of the blue *exp*. seemingly done without cause or reason

talk [one] into *phr v*. to persuade to do something

convince *v*. to cause to agree with or believe something

Reading

Read the following passage about aggressive marketing techniques.

Aggressive Marketing

   Companies that sell products to consumers need to market their products. There are often dozens of products for consumers to choose from. Producers use marketing to make their products stand out. Aggressive marketing tactics are those that actively look for customers and convince them to spend money. In highly competitive industries, the company that markets the most aggressively often finds the most success. Those companies that rely on basic advertising may suffer from weak sales.

| Analyzing | Answer the following questions. Give brief spoken responses to questions 2-4.

1   The passage defines aggressive marketing as
   Ⓐ the only alternative to basic advertising
   Ⓑ a way to compete against similar businesses
   Ⓒ too risky for most businesses to attempt
   Ⓓ used by dozens of kinds of businesses

2   What kind of company can benefit the most from aggressive marketing?

3   What is the goal of aggressive marketing?

4   **Critical Thinking:** How might aggressive marketing differ from basic advertising?

Listen to a short lecture related to the reading. Take notes on key words and specific information from the lecture.

Notes

02-61

Topic   *how businesses can use*

Detail 1   *example of a health club that wants to*

Detail 2

Key Words   *bold and energetic, consumers, new one every week,*

|Summarizing| In your own words, restate the main idea and the key points of the lecture.

Synthesizing

Give a brief spoken response to the questions based on the reading passage and the lecture.

1   Why does the professor use a health club as her example business?

2   Which actions by the health club would be considered aggressive marketing?

3   How does aggressive marketing benefit the health club in the example?

Speaking

Now give your spoken response for 60 seconds. You may use the guided response below to assist you.

The professor explains aggressive marketing. Explain the concept and how it is illustrated by the example.

▶ Guided Response

According to the passage, aggressive marketing means _____. It is especially useful

when _____. The professor explains that _____ can lead to

_____. She uses the example of _____.

Because there are many _____ and they are all _____,

it can be difficult to _____. The professor explains that a new health club

needs to _____. The example she uses is _____. The

coupons _____, and they offer _____. Some people

will _____, but others will become _____. Because of

_____, the health club now _____.

| Comparing | Listen to a sample response and compare it with yours.

02-62

⌐ **FOCUSING ON PRONUNCIATION** ⌐

Circle five words in the sample response that you have difficulty pronouncing. Write them in the space below.
Practice saying these words in a North American accent.

1 _____   2 _____   3 _____

4 _____   5 _____

Task 4 Animal Science: Venom

🔊 Vocabulary Take a few moments to review the vocabulary items that will appear in this task.

remarkable *adj.* worthy of attention or notice

toxin *n.* a poisonous substance

nerve *n.* a fiber in the body that conducts information to the muscles and organs

irritating *adj.* bothersome; slightly painful

deterrent *n.* something that prevents action

inject *v.* to push a liquid into something

stand no chance *exp.* to be unable to provide a challenge or defense

swallow [something] whole *exp.* to swallow something without chewing it

Listening

Listen to a lecture on the topic of venom. Take notes on key words and concepts in the lecture.

Notes

Topic *venom = substance used by animals for*

Detail 1 *bees use venom for self-defense against*

when it is stung, the bird's muscles

Detail 2

Key Words *physical trait, evolve, stinger,*

02-63

| **Summarizing** | Using your own words, summarize the topic of the lecture, describe how the professor explains the topic, and restate the key points.

Now give your spoken response for 60 seconds. You may use the guided response below to assist you.

Using points and examples from the lecture, explain what venom is and how it is used by animals.

▶ **Guided Response**

In the lecture, the professor explains _____ . Venom is
_____ . It makes the muscles _____ ,
so the animal _____ . The professor gives two examples that illustrate
_____ . He starts by speaking about bees. Bees have _____ .
When they are threatened, they _____ . This can be _____
such as a _____ . Therefore, many animals avoid _____ . Snakes show how
venom is used to _____ . Venomous snakes bite _____ . This
delivers the venom to the animals' bodies and _____ . The venom acts quickly, so the
animals _____ . Thanks to the venom, snakes can _____ .

| **Comparing** | Listen to a sample response and compare it with yours.

02-64

⌐ **FOCUSING ON PARAPHRASING** ⌐

Underline any three sentences in the sample response. Paraphrase each sentence in the space below. Then, practice saying each sentence with natural intonation.

-
-
-

Part C

Experiencing the TOEFL iBT Actual Tests

CONTINUE   VOLUME

03-01

Speaking Section Directions

 Make sure your headset is on.

This section measures your ability to speak about a variety of topics. You will answer four questions by speaking into the microphone. Answer as completely as possible.

In the first question, you will speak about familiar topics. Your response will be scored on your ability to speak clearly and coherently.

In the next two questions, you will first read a short reading passage. This passage will go away, and you will then listen to a talk on the same topic. You will be asked about the information you have read and heard. You will need to combine information from the reading passage and the talk to provide a complete answer. Your response will be scored on your ability to speak clearly and coherently and how accurately you convey information about what you read and heard.

In the last question, you will listen to part of a lecture. You will be asked about what you have heard. Your response will be scored on your ability to speak clearly and coherently and how accurately you convey information about what you heard.

You may take notes while you read and while you listen to the conversations and lectures. You may use your notes to help prepare your response.

Listen carefully to the directions for each question. The directions will not be written on the screen.

For each question you will be given a short time to prepare your response (15 to 30 seconds, depending on the question). A clock will show how much preparation time is remaining. When the preparation time is up, you will be told to begin your response. A clock will show how much response time is remaining. A message will appear on the screen when the response time has ended.

Task 1

03-02

Some people prefer to read news reports about bad or negative events. Others like reading about positive events. Which do you prefer and why? Give specific reasons and examples to support your opinion.

PREPARATION TIME
00:00:15

RESPONSE TIME
00:00:45

Task 2

03-03

Getting Rid of the Student Center Parking Lot

I am writing this letter to share my feelings about the student center parking lot. Ever since the new Bull Street parking garage was built, the student center parking lot has hardly been used. Therefore, it seems to me that the school should turn the parking lot into a green space for students. There are currently few green areas on campus, so this would enhance the environment at our school. For this reason, I strongly urge that the university get rid of the student center parking lot in favor of turning it into a small park for students.

The man expresses his opinion about turning the student center parking lot into a green space for students. State his opinion and explain the reasons he gives for holding that opinion.

PREPARATION TIME
00:00:30

RESPONSE TIME
00:00:60

Task 3

03-04

The Expectancy Effect

In psychology, there are experiments to test human behavior. Sometimes the participants or the scientists know what results to expect. This is called the expectancy effect. The test results can then be influenced by an experimenter's behavior, personality traits, or expectations. This often leads to test results that are inaccurate. The reason is that the participants or scientists ignore the actual results of their tests. Instead, they report the information they expected to be true.

The professor talks about how the expectations of scientists and participants in an experiment can affect the outcome. Explain how this relates to the expectancy effect.

PREPARATION TIME
00:00:30

RESPONSE TIME
00:00:60

Task 4

03-05

Using points and examples from the lecture, explain two ways in which animals use pheromones.

PREPARATION TIME
00:00:20

RESPONSE TIME
00:00:60

CONTINUE | VOLUME

03-06

Speaking Section Directions

 Make sure your headset is on.

This section measures your ability to speak about a variety of topics. You will answer four questions by speaking into the microphone. Answer as completely as possible.

In the first question, you will speak about familiar topics. Your response will be scored on your ability to speak clearly and coherently.

In the next two questions, you will first read a short reading passage. This passage will go away, and you will then listen to a talk on the same topic. You will be asked about the information you have read and heard. You will need to combine information from the reading passage and the talk to provide a complete answer. Your response will be scored on your ability to speak clearly and coherently and how accurately you convey information about what you read and heard.

In the last question, you will listen to part of a lecture. You will be asked about what you have heard. Your response will be scored on your ability to speak clearly and coherently and how accurately you convey information about what you heard.

You may take notes while you read and while you listen to the conversations and lectures. You may use your notes to help prepare your response.

Listen carefully to the directions for each question. The directions will not be written on the screen.

For each question you will be given a short time to prepare your response (15 to 30 seconds, depending on the question). A clock will show how much preparation time is remaining. When the preparation time is up, you will be told to begin your response. A clock will show how much response time is remaining. A message will appear on the screen when the response time has ended.

Task 1

03-07

Do you agree or disagree with the following statement? It is better to review class notes regularly rather than just during pre-test study sessions. Give specific reasons and examples to support your opinion.

PREPARATION TIME
00:00:15

RESPONSE TIME
00:00:45

Task 2

03-08

Cafeteria Hours to Be Extended

At the start of the fall semester, the hours of the cafeteria in Wilson Hall will be extended. The cafeteria usually closes at 8:00 PM. However, from Monday to Friday, the cafeteria will remain open until midnight. On Saturday and Sunday, it will stay open until 10:00 PM. Some hot foods may not be available after 8:00 PM. However, sandwiches, salads, and various snacks and desserts will be available until closing time. For more information regarding this change, visit the dining services office in room 101 of Salisbury Hall.

The woman expresses her opinion of the change in the school cafeteria's hours of operations. State her opinion and explain the reasons she gives for holding that opinion.

PREPARATION TIME
00:00:30

RESPONSE TIME
00:00:60

03-09

Latent Learning

Learning is the process of gaining new skills or knowledge through study. Oftentimes, learning occurs as the result of direct study. Other times, however, learning can occur without a person realizing it in a process known as latent learning. Latent learning happens when a person learns something subconsciously but does not immediately put this knowledge to use. The effect of the learning comes up later when the knowledge is needed. This is how children know how to set a dinner table or to clean dishes even if they have not been directly taught.

The professor describes a student knowing the route to school without having been taught it directly. Explain how this illustrates the concept of latent learning.

PREPARATION TIME
00:00:30

RESPONSE TIME
00:00:60

Task 4

03-10

Using points and examples from the lecture, explain two ways in which product packaging is appealing.

PREPARATION TIME
00:00:20

RESPONSE TIME
00:00:60

Appendix

MASTER
WORD LIST

Chapter 01

abolish *v.* to erase permanently; to get rid of

adapt *v.* to adjust based on a situation or environment

adversary *n.* an enemy; one who opposes

attract *v.* to cause to come near; to bring close

bargain *n.* a good price

consume *v.* to eat

debt *n.* the state of owing money

dues *n.* money owed for membership in a group or club

eager *adj.* showing strong interest

evolve *v.* to develop and change over time

expand one's horizons *exp.* to try something new

facts and figures *exp.* exact information about dates, numbers, and other data

mechanism *n.* a method or process for doing something

predator *n.* an animal that hunts another for food

proximity *n.* the state of being near something

put one's skills to the test *exp.* to use newly learned abilities

recall *n.* the act of remembering something

retention *n.* the ability to hold on to something

skipper *n.* the master of a boat or ship

snap *v.* to close quickly and forcefully

species *n.* a specific group of organisms

stuck in one's head *exp.* unable to forget

tricky *adj.* confusing; requiring caution and skill

Chapter 02

armor *n.* a hard, protective layer

budget *n.* a plan for the use of money

cigarette butt *n.* the leftover portion of a used cigarette

desired *adj.* wanted; hoped for

deter *v.* to cause to avoid; to discourage action

differ *v.* to be different from

do one's part *exp.* to participate equally

enroll *v.* to join, especially a school or university

filthy *adj.* extremely dirty

herbivorous *adj.* plant-eating

housekeeper *n.* a person who cleans rooms, especially at a hotel

ingest *v.* to swallow and absorb

injure *v.* to cause serious pain or damage

lateral *adj.* moving sideways; horizontal

logic *n.* a systematic way of thinking to solve problems

outcome *n.* a result

pesticide *n.* a chemical that kills certain insects

potential *adj.* possible

session *n.* a time period used for a specific purpose

staff *n.* the employees working at a company

thorn *n.* a sharp, pointy part of a plant's stem

turnoff *n.* something that causes dislike or disinterest

whereas *conj.* while at the same time; on the other hand

Chapter 03

bronze *n.* a metal mixture of copper and tin

carve *v.* to cut a shape into a hard substance

cement *n.* a building material that dries rock hard

chip away *phr v.* to cut small pieces from a larger object

close [one's] doors *exp.* to go out of business

collaboration *n.* working together

dim *adj.* not bright; slightly dark

do the trick *exp.* to accomplish a goal

flexible *adj.* able to be moved or bent easily

letdown *n.* something that is disappointing

marble *n.* a kind of rock used in architecture and art

master *v.* to become an expert

medieval *adj.* relating to the period between the 5th and 15th centuries

no matter which *exp.* shows that all choices are equal

passive *adj.* receiving action without responding

peasant *n.* a person in the lowest social class

pose *n.* a way of positioning the body

precision *n.* the state of being exact or accurate

promotional *adj.* in a way that advertises an idea, product, or service

propose *v.* to suggest or recommend an idea

reenact *v.* to perform a historical story, as in a play

role-play *v.* to do a learning exercise during which students act as characters

sculpt *v.* to shape clay or rocks into a 3-D form

student council *n.* a campus group that represents student interests

tradeoff *n.* a situation during which a person gives up one thing to gain another

turn [something] around *phr v.* to improve the quality or performance of

Chapter 04

altered *ad.* changed; different

aquatic *adj.* relating to water

burrow *v.* to dig a hole or passage in the ground

cattle *n.* a group of cows

classic *adj.* typical; of a well-known type

cocoon *n.* a protective covering made by an animal

coral reef *n.* a large, underwater rock-like structure

detriment *n.* harm to the health or wellbeing of

dormant *adj.* inactive; being in a state of inactivity

exclude *v.* to leave out; to remove from a list of options

institute *v.* to put into effect

like shooting fish in a barrel *exp.* easy to do

mess *n.* something that is disorganized

mutualism *n.* a relationship in which both organisms benefit

parasitism *n.* a relationship in which one organism benefits but causes harm to another

precipitation *n.* rain, snow, ice, or hail that falls from the sky

shed *v.* to lose; to get rid of

starving *adj.* extremely hungry

thrive *v.* to prosper; to do very well; to be successful

vegetation *n.* plant life

advantageous *adj.* providing some benefits or advantages

alert *v.* to warn of approaching danger or action

alongside *adv.* together with; in cooperation with

committee *n.* a group that makes decisions for an organization

complementary *adj.* making something perfect or whole

concentrate *v.* to meet in a common center

conduct *v.* to carry out; to perform

expel *v.* to force or drive away

have [it] all worked out *exp.* to have answers for or a plan to solve a challenge

infectious *adj.* able to be spread from one person to another

is no joke *exp.* shows that something is difficult

kick out *phr v.* to force to leave

lit *n.* an abbreviation for "literature"

lone *adj.* by oneself; with no others

microorganism *n.* an organism so small that it cannot be seen by the naked eye

never-ending *adj.* continuing without any sign of stopping

observe *v.* to watch carefully

premise *n.* the basis for an argument

rid *v.* to remove from a location or system

roam *v.* to move about in no particular direction

strategy *n.* a plan of action

swell up *phr v.* to expand abnormally

thesis *n.* a lengthy essay used to prove academic achievement

undergraduate *adj.* relating to the basic four-year course at a university

alarmed *adj.* surprised and upset

all walks of life *exp.* various social groups

alpha male *n.* the most dominant male in a group

behavior *n.* how a person or animal acts

billboard *n.* a large roadside sign used for advertising

break *n.* a period of rest between classes or work

challenge *v.* to threaten; to provoke one into a fight

cologne *n.* a scented spray used by men

conscious *adj.* concerned about; actively aware of

cruise trip *n.* a holiday vacation on a luxury ship

diet *n.* the food that one eats

growl *v.* to make a low, steady sound, especially like one made by angry dogs

hardly *adv.* almost not; barely

identify *v.* to learn the identity of

migrate *v.* to move from one place to another, often for food or mating

mutual *adj.* shared in common

overwhelmingly *adv.* extremely in effect or strength

segment *n.* one part of a whole

social system *n.* a set of cultural and structural elements in a group

target *v.* to aim at or focus on

territory *n.* the land claimed by an animal or group of animals

advisor *n.* an expert who gives advice

agriculture *n.* the act of growing food for humans to eat

brutal *adj.* showing no kindness or mercy

distinguish *v.* to separate as different from something else

fee *n.* money a person pays for a service

general *n.* a high-ranking leader in a military force

grid *n.* a pattern of squares made by crossing lines

flash *v.* to occur suddenly and briefly

habit *n.* a regular activity a person does

invest *v.* to spend money on something in the hope of making more money in the future

landmark *adj.* highly important or significant

minimum *adj.* being the least possible

mixed feelings *phr n.* a partly positive and partly negative reaction to something

momentarily *adv.* for a brief time

pastime *n.* a free-time activity; something a person does that makes time pass pleasantly

recover *v.* to get back something that was spent or lost

rent *v.* to charge money to let a person use something for a certain amount of time

soldier *n.* a person who serves in an army

subconscious *adj.* unnoticed by the active part of the mind

victorious *adj.* having won a battle or contest

Chapter 08

across the board *exp.* including all items or members of a group

convince *v.* to cause to agree with or believe something

deterrent *n.* something that prevents action

distraction *n.* something that takes away one's attention

dozens *n.* a large, unspecific number

enhance *v.* to change in order to make better

I'm not following you *exp.* an that shows someone does not understand

inject *v.* to push a liquid into something

irritating *adj.* bothersome; slightly painful

nerve *n.* a fiber in the body that conducts information to the muscles and organs

out of the blue *exp.* seemingly done without cause or reason

remarkable *adj.* worthy of attention or notice

stand no chance *exp.* to be unable to provide a challenge or defense

stand out *phr v.* to be noticed amongst a large group

swallow [something] whole *exp.* to swallow something without chewing it

tactic *n.* a plan for achieving a goal

talk [one] into *phr v.* to persuade to do something

toxin *n.* a poisonous substance

MEMO

MEMO

MEMO

MEMO

MEMO

MEMO

MEMO

MEMO

TOEFL® MAP

Speaking

New TOEFL® Edition

Intermediate

Scripts and Answer Key

DARAKWON

TOEFL® MAP Speaking

New TOEFL® Edition

Speaking

Intermediate

Scripts and Answer Key

 DARAKWON

■ Chapter | **01** Independent Speaking

Task 1 Trying New Food at Restaurants

Brainstorming   p.26

| Critical Thinking |

Answers may vary.

1   I could love it and have a new favorite food.

2   It is not important because you can be happy eating the food you already enjoy.

3   You can expect that it is something you like, but it will also not be interesting or exciting.

Organizing   p.28

Answers may vary.

> **My Choice:** *order a new dish*
>
> **Reason 1:** *more exciting than eating something predictable – like exploring a new land*
>
> **Reason 2:** *makes me like a world traveler – can expand my interest in other cultures through food*

Speaking   p.28

▶ **Guided Response 1 Order the Same Dish**   02-01

When I go to restaurants, I usually order *something that I have tried before*. There are a couple of reasons why I *like to eat the same dish*. For one thing, ordering *something I know that I like* lets me *be sure that I'm going to enjoy the meal and not waste my money*. Because I have ordered it before, I know that *it's going to be an enjoyable meal even though it is not new or exciting*. The other reason is that when I try new food, it makes me feel *nervous that I won't like it*. The dish might be delicious, or it might be disgusting, so *the best way to ensure a good meal is by ordering something that I've tried before*. That's why I always order *the same dish* when I go to restaurants.

▶ **Guided Response 2 Order a New Dish**   02-02

I don't eat out often, so whenever I go out, I want to *take the chance to try something new and different*. The main reason is that I can *have a meal and an*

adventure. When you order the same thing, it is always *a predictable taste that you can already imagine before the food comes*. But a new dish can be *like exploring a new territory*. That makes eating out *exciting* than usual. In addition to that, I think that ordering a new dish *prepares me for traveling abroad one day*. I can learn about *other cultures by trying their food*, and I can expand my *tastes and learn to like new kinds of flavors*. So just by eating food, I can *feel like a world traveler*.

■ Chapter | **01** Integrated Speaking

Task 2 Campus Sailing Club

Reading   p.30

| Analyzing |

1   Ⓐ

2   The lake's proximity shows that it is easy to access a place to go sailing.

3   The cost is 130 dollars per semester, and the money is used for buying equipment and harbor space.

4   Answers may vary.
    That person may enjoy doing outdoor activities in his or her free time.

Listening   p.31

Scripts & Notes 02-03

M: Hey, I think I found the club I'm going to join this year. Just call me Skipper John.

W: Okay, Skipper John, but you don't know anything about boats. You can't even swim.

M: It says here that beginners are welcome. I'm always up for a new challenge. Since I've never been on a boat, I could learn a lot.

W: You do love trying new things. What about the cost though?

M: It's only 130 dollars a semester. I think that's a bargain.

W: But you work on the weekends at your part-time job. The club meets on Saturdays.

M: Well, I've been thinking about getting a student loan. Then, I could work fewer hours and have more free time.

W: Do you think that's a wise choice? You'll be in debt after you graduate.

M: Yeah, but I want to enjoy myself while I'm at university. You're only young once, you know.

W: I guess you're right. You can always pay off your loans later.

> **Notes**
>
> The man is _interested_ in the announcement.
>
> **Reason 1** _wants to try new things; loves a challenge_
>
> **Reason 2** _says that he should try new things while he is young; may quit his part-time job to make time for sailing_
>
> **Key Words and Details** _try new things, bargain, student loan, only young once_

Synthesizing
p.31

1 He is referring to the announcement about the sailing club because he wants to join it.

2 She thinks the man would not like it and does not have time for it.

3 He would need to quit his job and take out a student loan.

Speaking
p.32

▶ **Guided Response**
02-04

The speakers are discussing _an announcement for a sailing club at the university_. According to the announcement, _students can join for 130 dollars a semester and go sailing twice a month_. The man is interested _in the club_ and says _that he might join it_. His first reason for having that opinion is _that he enjoys trying new things_. The woman reminds him that _he cannot swim_, and he says _that he likes to attempt new challenges_. He then addresses _the issue of money_. Joining the club would mean he wouldn't be able to _work as often_. He thinks he could _quit his job_ and _take out a student loan_. That way, he could enjoy _his time at the university_. So he is considering _joining the club_ because he wants to _try something new and challenging_ and he thinks it will help him _make the most of his time while he is young_.

Task 3 Psychology: Memory Tricks

Reading
p.33

| **Analyzing** |

1 ⓒ

2 A mnemonic device is a trick that helps a person remember information.

3 The devices will increase students' chances of remembering important information.

4 Answers may vary.
There is no context for the information.

Listening
p.34

Script & Notes 02-05

Professor: Now, I know that I've given you guys a pretty big list of words to memorize. Don't worry though. I'm going to show you how to use mnemonic devices to get these words stuck in your head.

One of my favorite tricks is to create rhymes. You guys all know when Columbus sailed to the Americas, right? How do you remember that date? _In 1492, Columbus sailed the ocean blue_. It's a silly rhyme, but it works. So how can you use this with your vocabulary list? Let's look at one of the words on your list: adversary. It means your enemy or someone who is against you. Thus, _my adversary is big and scary_. I bet you'll never forget that word now.

And, ah . . . okay, on to the next mnemonic device. This one takes a little bit of creativity. When you see a difficult word, try to imagine a picture that represents the word and its meaning. For example, the word "abolish" can be a tricky one. It means to get rid of something—usually something bad. And it sounds like "polish," right? So just think of a person polishing shoes to get rid of spots or stains. He's abolishing his shoes' dirtiness.

⬤ Notes

Topic *mnemonic devices and how they can be used for studying*

Detail 1 *first device = rhyming*

ex: In 1492, Columbus sailed the ocean blue.; My adversary is big and scary.

Detail 2 *next device = mental image*

ex: abolish → polish; polish shoes; remove stains; abolish = remove

Key Words and Details *in 1492, silly rhyme, enemy, creativity, spots or stains*

Synthesizing   p.34

1   The professor explains the concept by giving examples of mnemonic devices and how to use them.

2   The information in the reading passage is difficult to understand without concrete examples, like those in the lecture.

3   The examples help the listener understand exactly what a mnemonic device is.

Speaking   p.35

▶ **Guided Response**   02-06

The topic of the reading is *mnemonic devices*. These are *strategies that students can use to memorize lots of information*. According to the passage, using a mnemonic device helps students *not to forget facts and figures*. The professor elaborates on the topic by *giving two examples of mnemonic devices for memorizing vocabulary*. The first one he talks about is *rhyming*. By creating sentences that rhyme, *it can be easy to remember a word*. He gives the example of "*my adversary is big and scary*." The professor then introduces a second mnemonic device: *creating images in your mind*. He explains that *creating images that explain a word* can help you *remember it*. The example he uses is for the word "*abolish*." Since it sounds like "*polish*" and means *to get rid of something*, he says to picture someone *polishing dirty shoes*.

Task 4 Life Science: Mimicry

Listening   p.36

Script & Notes 02-07

Professor: One way that plants and animals have adapted to their environments is through a process known as mimicry. This is when an organism has evolved to look like—or mimic—another animal or plant.

Mimicry commonly serves as a defensive mechanism and protects the creature from predators. Usually this shows up as a weak or defenseless animal mimicking a poisonous or dangerous animal. The idea is that a predator will think the prey animal is dangerous and will therefore not attack it. Defensive mimicry can be seen in butterflies. A few different species have evolved to look like the plain tiger butterfly. Why does this help the mimic? Well, most predators have learned to avoid the plain tiger because of its taste. When attacked, it releases a terrible tasting liquid. So birds and other predators don't try to eat any butterfly that could be a plain tiger.

But mimicry does more than provide protection from harm. Some creatures use it as a way to hide from or attract their prey. So a predator looks like a harmless or even attractive plant or animal. Think about Venus flytraps. They have these giant, ah, "mouths" that are full of sharp teeth. But when they open up, they look like pink flowers. Bees and other animals go right into the flytrap's mouth in search of food. But instead of finding food, they become meals for the flytrap, which snaps its mouth shut and consumes the helpless creatures.

⬤ Notes

Topic *mimicry = animal or plant evolving to look like something else*

Detail 1 *defensive mimicry = weak animal looking like stronger animal for protection*

ex: plain tiger butterfly; bad taste = predators avoid

Detail 2 *another kind of mimicry helps predators attract prey*

ex: Venus flytrap looks like a flower; attracts bees and other creatures

Key Words *defensive mechanism, weak animal, terrible taste, avoid, attract, Venus flytrap*

▶ **Guided Response**   02-08

The topic of the *lecture is mimicry*. This is something that *plants and animals* have evolved over time. It is a way for them to *survive in their natural environment*. The professor explains that mimicry works in two ways. One way is *to help the organism avoid being attacked and eaten by* predators. This point is illustrated with the example of *butterflies*. According to the lecture, the butterfly known as the *plain tiger* is not *tasty to predators* because of *a disgusting liquid it releases when it is attacked*. Because of this, butterflies that look like the plain tiger *are also safe from attack*. Mimicry helps them *survive in the wild*. The other way mimicry works is to help predators *catch their prey*. This is also explained with an example: *Venus flytraps*. The Venus flytrap opens *its mouth and looks like a pink flower*, so some creatures *think it is safe to walk in in search of food*. The creature is *tricked by the mimicry*, and the *Venus flytrap has a meal*.

▮▬ Chapter | 02 **Independent Speaking**

Task 1 Ability vs. Hard Work

Brainstorming   p.40

| Critical Thinking |

Answers may vary.

1   Some people take lessons, but others teach themselves.

2   Mozart was a successful composer who taught himself to play instruments.

3   I would probably try to improve through lessons if I had no natural skill.

Organizing   p.42

Answers may vary.

My Choice: *natural ability*

Reason 1: *successful artists may have trained, but their natural ability is why they are successful*

Reason 2: *without natural talent, people will give up*

ex: I stopped studying the violin because I was terrible, even after taking lessons.

▶ **Guided Response 1**   **Natural Ability**   02-09

Hard work is important for any profession, but I think *natural ability is more important*. Every person is born with *some kind of ability*. Successful artists are *just normal people* who have found a *special skill that they were born with* and developed into a career. Sure, they may have trained, but without *the ability to paint or draw, they would never be successful*. Furthermore, if someone has no natural ability, that person will probably *give up on studying his or her craft* instead of continuing it. People like to learn skills that *they are naturally good at*. For example, I tried to learn *how to play the violin*. I was terrible even after taking lessons, so *I gave up learning the violin* and decided to practice *playing the drum* instead.

▶ **Guided Response 2**   **Hard Work**   02-10

When it comes to being a successful artist, I think that *hard work is the most important factor*. One way to prove this is to look at *famous artists throughout history* as an example. *One artist is Michelangelo, who was* a successful artist during *the Renaissance*. This artist may have been born with skill, but *he also spent many years studying at an art academy*. Without this training, *he may not have learned the technical aspects that allowed him to become such a great painter*. To look at a broader example, there are *training institutes* for all fields of art. These have existed for *several centuries and even millennia*. This shows that, historically, people think that artists *must learn to master the basic forms and skills*. In other words, natural ability alone cannot *lead to great success*.

▮▬ Chapter | 02 **Integrated Speaking**

Task 2 Campus Clean-up Day

Reading   p.44

| Analyzing |

1   ⓓ

2   These are examples that the student uses to support her opinion that the campus is dirty.

3   The writer thinks that students should organize a campus clean-up day.

4   Answers may vary.
    Students may feel that it is unfair for them to clean up the campus grounds.

M: I think this student makes a good point. The campus is filthy. I would be embarrassed to show it to potential students.

W: Yeah, I agree with her on that. The campus certainly needs to be cleaned up.

M: So are you going to sign up for a clean-up day?

W: Well, this is where our opinions differ. I want the campus to be cleaned but not by students.

M: What do you mean?

W: Our focus as students is to learn. We didn't enroll in university to do clean-up jobs. We need to concentrate on our class work.

M: Sure, but having a dirty campus doesn't help us concentrate.

W: That's right. The school definitely needs to do something about it.

M: So what do you suggest?

W: The school should hire professional cleaners to do the job. There are cleaning services that can do a great job.

M: And since they are professionals, they could do a better job than students.

W: Exactly. I say that the university should hire a professional cleaning crew to clean up once a month.

> **Notes**
>
> The woman _disagrees_ with the letter.
>
> **Reason 1** _thinks students should focus on their studies, not on cleaning the campus_
>
> **Reason 2** _says that the school should hire professionals, who can do a better job_
>
> **Key Words and Details** _opinions differ, focus, concentrate, class work, professional cleaners, cleaning crew_

1   She agrees that the campus needs to be cleaned up.

2   She does not want to help because she feels it is not the job of students to clean the campus.

3   He offers a reason why a cleaning crew would be

better than a student clean-up day.

The man and the woman are talking about _a letter to the editor_ that addresses the problem of _litter on a university's campus_. The letter writer is upset about _the state of cleanliness on her campus_. She points to _cigarette butts and empty soda cans_ as examples of the litter that can be found on campus and argues that students _should organize a clean-up day_. The woman sees the letter and _agrees that the campus is dirty_, but she does not agree with _the suggestion in the letter_. She does not feel that students _should be responsible for cleaning the campus_. She says that a student's goal is _to focus on getting good grades and learning_, not _on cleaning up a campus_. Instead, she argues, the university should _hire a professional cleaning crew to regularly maintain the campus_. These people would _be more effective cleaners_ since they are professionals, and their work would allow students to _continue to focus on education_.

▶ Chapter | **02** Integrated Speaking

Task 3 Plant Biology: Self-Defense

| Analyzing |

1   ⒝

2   The passage briefly describes the problem and then defines two types of self-defense.

3   Chemicals cause injury from the inside while physical defenses inflict pain from outside the body.

4   Answers may vary.
    They have different predators, so they need different ways of surviving.

Professor: You may think that plants are defenseless compared to animals. I mean, they can't run away from predators, can they? But that doesn't mean they can't defend themselves. Whereas animals typically have only physical defensive mechanisms, such as speed or sharp teeth, plants have a couple of self-defense options.

I'll explain what I mean with a very common example: the tobacco plant. Humans like to use tobacco in cigarettes, but we have another use for it: pesticides. The reason is that the chemical it produces—nicotine—can make a lot of insects and animals sick. These predators, over time, have learned not to eat tobacco plants. Even humans may become sick after ingesting nicotine.

Now, let's turn our attention to physical defenses, called mechanical defenses. How can a plant's shape deter predators? Imagine eating a raspberry plant, which is covered in tiny thorns. It would cut your mouth up, and you'd never eat it again, right? Other plants grow sharp or smooth leaves that are difficult to eat. Another mechanical defense, as seen in the coconut tree, is to grow a thick, ah, "armor" around its fruit. It's extremely difficult to get through a coconut's shell to reach its fruit.

> **Notes**

Topic *plants that use self-defense to avoid being eaten*

Detail 1 *chemical defense = the production of chemicals that can make animals sick or injured*

ex: tobacco plant has nicotine, a kind of pesticide; animals avoid eating

Detail 2 *mechanical defense = plant's shape causes physical pain*

ex: raspberry plant – painful thorns; sharp or smooth leaves – hard to eat; coconut tree – armor around fruit

Key Words *physical defense, tobacco, pesticide, nicotine, plant's shape, tiny thorns, armor*

Synthesizing   p.48

1   The professor gives several examples of self-defense mechanisms in plants.

2   The examples help the students understand what the difference between chemical and mechanical defenses is.

3   Defense is usually thought of as an animal ability, and she wants to show that not only animals can defend themselves.

Speaking   p.49

▶ **Guided Response**   02-14

The professor begins the lecture by comparing *plants and animals*. She says that, like animals, plants have evolved *different ways to defend themselves*. She explains with the first example of *the tobacco plant*. These plants have *some predators* that want to eat them. However, because of *the chemical nicotine*, predators *avoid eating tobacco plants*. They *would get sick* if they ate the plants. This example *illustrates* the concept of *chemical defense* introduced in the reading passage. The professor then brings up *mechanical defenses*. The reading passage says that this is *a physical trait that is* used by plants. One example the professor gives is of *raspberry plants*. These grow *sharp thorns on them*, which, if eaten, *can injure an animal's mouth*. Because of that, predators *do not want to eat raspberry plants*. Another example of *mechanical defense* is the *coconut tree*, which grows *a hard, protective shell* in order to protect its fruit. It is almost impossible for predators to *eat coconuts because they cannot break through the armor*.

 Chapter | **02** Integrated Speaking

Task 4 Business: Lateral Thinking

Listening   p.50

Script & Notes 02-15

Professor: As future business leaders, you're going to need some basic problem-solving strategies for when things go wrong. Logic tells you to solve problems by working in steps. You picture the desired outcome and work backward to the problem. But what if this doesn't work? You may find that none of your solutions is very attractive. That's when you need to use lateral thinking.

The term means to approach problems from a different direction. It involves using creativity to solve problems. There are different methods, but a great way is to brainstorm. And don't think you should only talk to your managing staff. Any of the employees could have an idea that leads to a brilliant solution to your problem.

Let me tell you about a friend of mine. She's a hotel manager in a small town. Guests enjoyed the hotel, but they had a common complaint: The elevator was too slow for them. Guests would wait two or sometimes three minutes for the elevator to come. The two most obvious solutions were to fix the elevator or to install a new one. Both of these options were too expensive. She simply did not have the budget to fix or replace the elevator. So she had a brainstorming session with all of her employees. One of the housekeepers had an idea: Install a television next to the elevator. It was a cheap idea and easy to test. Guess what. It worked. The guests were so busy watching television that they didn't notice their waiting time. That's a perfect example of lateral thinking.

Notes

Topic *lateral thinking = attempting to solve problems from a different direction rather than by trying to solve them step by step*

Detail 1 *happens by using creativity and brainstorming; should make use of everyone on the staff, not only management*

Detail 2 *professor's personal story of hotel manager and broken elevator; put TV by elevator instead of fixing it*

Key Words *problem-solving, working in steps, creativity, brainstorm, managing staff, obvious solutions, housekeeper*

Speaking
p.51

▶ **Guided Response** 02-16

The lecture is about *lateral thinking*, which is *a method that business managers can use to solve problems* when working in logical steps does not *produce a good solution*. Unlike logical thinking, lateral thinking comes from *another angle* and uses *creativity to solve problems*. The professor explains that this can be done by *having a brainstorming session with a person's staff*. He cautions that a business manager should *consult all staff members*, not *just managers*, because anybody could *have a good idea*. He tells a personal story to *drive home this point and to illustrate the concept of lateral thinking*. His friend, *a hotel manager*, had a *slow elevator* that guests *complained about*. There was no money to *replace or fix it*, so the hotel manager *consulted her staff*. A housekeeper suggested *putting a TV by the elevator to distract the guests at the hotel*. This solution reduced *guest complaints about waiting on the elevator*, and it showed how *a creative idea works better than using logical steps* to fix a problem.

Task 1 Taking a Vacation

Brainstorming
p.54

| Critical Thinking |

Answers may vary.

1   When I travel, I mostly like to relax and get some rest. However, I also enjoy sightseeing when I visit new places.

2   I think that staying in a comfortable place makes traveling more enjoyable. Bad traffic and big crowds of people make traveling less enjoyable.

3   The last time I went on a trip, I stayed at a resort with my family. We stayed there because my parents just wanted to relax at the beach.

Organizing
p.56

Answers may vary.

> **My Choice:** *hotel*
>
> **Reason 1:** *convenient – in a good location; can do lots of sightseeing*
>
> **Reason 2:** *inexpensive – don't want to spend too much money on accommodations*

Speaking
p.56

▶ **Guided Response 1 Go Camping** 02-17

I would prefer to *go camping than to stay at a hotel or resort*. One reason I prefer camping is *that I love to spend time outdoors*. There is nothing better than *hiking through a forest, fishing in a lake, and sleeping in a tent*. I went camping *with my parents a couple of months ago*. We spent three days in a forest and had the best trip. In addition, camping *lets you get away from crowds of people*. I live in a big city, and *it can be overwhelming at times*. There are just *too many people there*. When we went camping, we did not *see a single person until we left the forest*. It was so relaxing to *get away from everyone* and *to have a quiet trip*.

▶ **Guided Response 2 Stay at a Hotel** 02-18

Of the three choices, I would rather *stay at a hotel when I travel*. The main reason is that *hotels are convenient*. For example, *they are close to restaurants, shopping centers, and tourist sites*. That means *I can easily go sightseeing if I stay at a hotel*. On my last trip, the hotel my family stayed at *was near several museums*. We could *walk to them from our hotel*, which was convenient. Another reason is that *hotels are usually inexpensive*. I don't want to *spend too much money on accommodations*. We stayed at *a budget hotel on our last trip*. We used the money that we saved to *have some nice dinners and to rent a car to travel around more easily*. That made our trip much better.

▶ Chapter | 03 Integrated Speaking

Task 2 Campus Coffee Shop Closing

Reading

p.58

| Analyzing |

1 ⓒ

2 It advertised, hosted events, and gave discounts.

3 The passage says that sales at the coffee shop have always been slow.

4 Answers may vary.
  A student who enjoys going to the coffee shop might be upset that his or her favorite location is closing.

Listening

p.59

Script & Notes 02-19

M: What a letdown. The Scholars Café is the only place on campus where I can get a good cup of coffee.

W: I understand the university's position. There aren't enough customers.

M: But it doesn't have to be that way. Management could make some changes and turn the place around.

W: What would you suggest be done?

M: Well, the school wants it to be a place to study, right? What place do you know that is good for studying?

W: Hmm . . . The library?

M: Right. And the library has great lighting. It's very easy to read in there. The coffee shop's lighting is too dim though.

W: So if better lighting were installed, students would be more likely to study there.

M: Exactly. And if they want to attract groups, they need new seating. The chairs are not very comfortable, and the tables are small.

W: You think they need to put in new furniture?

M: Sure. Some big, comfortable chairs for group discussion and larger tables for group study sessions would do the trick.

▶ Notes ◀

The man *disagrees* with the decision in the announcement.

Reason 1 *believes the coffee shop could stay open if it had better lighting for students who want to study*

Reason 2 *the coffee shop also needs bigger tables and more comfortable chairs to encourage students to study there*

Key Words and Details *university's position, lighting, too dim, new seating, group discussion, do the trick*

Synthesizing

p.59

1 He is supporting his opinion that the coffee shop does not need to close.

2 He says it is the only place on campus to get good coffee.

3 He thinks the lighting is bad and the furniture is uncomfortable and not good for group study sessions.

Speaking

p.60

▶ **Guided Response**   02-20

The conversation is about an announcement that *says the campus coffee shop will close due to low sales*. The student council intended the coffee shop as *a place for students to study*. However, students *are not studying there*, so *the shop will close*. The man thinks that *closing the shop* is unnecessary and that *sales would improve* if the coffee shop *were improved to make it a better study environment*. His first idea is that *the lighting should be improved*. The current lighting is *too low*, which makes it *difficult to study in*. The man says the lighting should *be like that of the library*, which is *a favorite study location*.

The other idea he has is *to improve the seating*. He thinks that more *comfortable chairs and large tables for study groups* would encourage people to *study there*. Based on these ideas, the man thinks *the coffee shop does not need to be closed*.

Chapter | **03** Integrated Speaking

Task 3 Education: Active Learning

Reading

p.61

| **Analyzing** |

1 Ⓐ

2 Active learning requires student participation, such as discussions or presentations.

3 Students have better memory retention.

4 Answers may vary.
Role-playing exercises are an example of active learning.

Listening

p.62

Script & Notes 02-21

Professor: When I was a student in university, one of my professors had a creative approach to teaching history. At first, I wasn't excited to take a history class. We all know that memorizing all those dates and facts can be boring. But in this course, we took a different approach. The professor had us role-play the material that we studied. This class was on medieval Europe. Each student had a role: peasant, landowner, king, sailor, and so forth. Each month, we used the information from the textbook to reenact an event from the time period. It was great fun, and we all learned a lot of history.

Years later, I realized my professor had used active learning. Now, active learning doesn't have to be role-playing; that was just one example. No matter which technique you use, the result is always the same: Students actually learn. They don't just memorize facts but actually absorb the information. Active learning produces excellent results in all subjects. The downside, however, is that active learning requires a lot of time. Because the techniques involve more than reading and lecturing, exercises take longer to complete. Therefore, the number of topics you can cover during a semester is

limited, so there is a tradeoff.

Notes

Topic *how active learning can be used to improve learning experience*

Detail 1 *personal story about role-playing used to learn about medieval European history*

students had various roles (peasant, landowner, king, etc.) and acted out scenes from history

Detail 2 *requires a lot of work but lets you learn a topic instead of memorizing facts*

drawback = time that it takes limits the number of topics that can be taught

Key Words *creative approach, medieval Europe, had a role, to reenact an event, actually learn, absorb the information, excellent result, requires a lot of time*

Synthesizing

p.62

1 She starts with an example to introduce the topic in a way that is easy to understand.

2 The lecture clarifies what is meant by exercises and activities that involve active learning.

3 It is a tradeoff because even though it is effective, it limits the number of topics that can be used.

Speaking

p.63

▶ **Guided Response** 02-22

Active learning is the name given to *new learning methods that directly involve the students*. They differ from *traditional learning methods* in which students simply *read and listen to lectures*, and they have been shown to be more effective for *remembering information*. Active learning can be one of various methods, such as *class discussions* and *group projects*. The professor illustrates the concept by *discussing an event from her time in university*. In a *medieval European history* class, the professor decided to *make the students do role-playing*. Each student *had a part to play*. For example, some students *were peasants*, another was *king*, and others were *sailors*. The students *acted out stories from history*. The professor said that the role-playing *transformed a boring history class into something interesting and exciting*. She also states that the students *learned a lot from the process*, which demonstrates *the point about effectiveness* mentioned in the reading.

● Chapter | 03 Integrated Speaking

Task 4 The Arts: Sculpture

Listening   p.64

Script & Notes 02-23

Professor: Looking at Michelangelo's *David*, it's hard to believe that such a detailed and beautiful sculpture started as a giant block of marble. But that's just what it was. Michelangelo chipped away at a marble block until his work was done. This is a technique of sculpting called subtractive sculpture. Subtractive sculpture is usually considered the most difficult technique to master. The artist cannot make a mistake. It requires total precision. That's why most artists start with clay. They use clay to make a model. Then, when they carve the rock, they can use the clay model to see exactly where they need to cut. Michelangelo used this technique when he carved most of his sculptures. It was not until late in his life, when he had become a master of carving, that he made sculptures without using clay models.

The other sculpture method is, as you may have guessed, additive. In additive sculpture, the artist works by adding clay until the desired look is achieved. Clay is very easy to work with. It allows the artist the chance to fix mistakes or make changes to the sculpture. After the sculpture is finished, it is set in bronze, cement, or some other strong material. Additive sculpture has several benefits. As I mentioned, it is more flexible than subtractive sculpture. It also provides more options. With subtractive sculpture, the artwork must be contained within the size of the original rock. You cannot have arms reaching out, for example. But with additive sculpture, any pose is possible. These factors give artists more freedom of expression, so most artists today practice additive sculpture.

Notes

Topic *two types of sculpture: subtractive and additive*

Detail 1 *subtractive sculpture = artist starts with a block and chips away pieces*

most difficult type because it requires total precision and the artist cannot make a mistake

Detail 2 *additive sculpture = the artist builds a sculpture with clay and sets it in a hard substance to make it permanent*

gives the artist more options: any pose is possible, such as arms stretching out

Key Words *marble block, total precision, clay model, master of carving, flexible, give artists more freedom*

Speaking   p.65

▶ **Guided Response**   02-24

The professor gives a lecture about *two techniques for creating sculptures*. The professor starts by explaining *subtractive sculpture*, a technique that was used by *Michelangelo*. To use this technique, the artist starts with *a block of marble* and *chips away at it with tools*. According to the professor, it is difficult *to master, and the artist must be completely accurate*. With just one mistake, *the sculpture can be ruined*. Therefore, most artists use *clay models*. These help the artists *know where they want to chip away at the rock*. The professor then describes *additive sculpture*, which differs from *subtractive sculpture* in that it is easier to do. The artist begins with *some clay* and adds *more and more clay until the sculpture is how the artist wants it*. Once the artist *is happy with the design*, the sculpture is finished with *a hard material, such as cement or bronze*. Most artists *prefer to use additive sculpture* because it *is more forgiving of mistakes* and *gives them more options for poses and shapes*.

Task 1 Preferred Study Environment

Brainstorming p.68

| Critical Thinking |

Answers may vary.

1 Music hurts my concentration because I get distracted and pay attention to the music.

2 Yes, any kind of noise, such as shouting and construction work, can hurt my concentration.

3 One cannot study effectively if one is uncomfortable.

Organizing p.70

Answers may vary.

> **My Choice:** *with music*
>
> **Reason 1:** *better concentration – not distracted by my thoughts or daydreaming*
>
> **Reason 2:** *improves endurance – helps me not get antsy*

Speaking p.70

▶ **Guided Response 1 Quiet** 02-25

When I study, I like *to have complete silence*. In my experience, listening to music while studying can *make me focus on the music too much*. My studying is *not as effective* because of my lower level of concentration. Because of this, listening to music while studying *can lead to lower grades*, which is something that *I definitely want to avoid*. I have tried to *listen to music when studying* in the past. I listened to *jazz* music and even *classical music*, which my teacher recommended. My test scores *ended up being lower than normal*. Since that time, I decided *to study in total silence*. As a result, my grades *have risen back to their normal levels*.

▶ **Guided Response 2 With Music** 02-26

I'm the kind of person that likes *to listen to music all the time*. When I study, *I do not change my behavior*. I listen to music when I study first because it *helps me to concentrate better on my studies*. When the room is quiet, my thoughts *begin to fill my head, and I get distracted by daydreaming*. But with music on, I can *keep my mind active with the beat and melodies*. My thoughts no longer *distract me*. Music does more than

that. It also helps me *study for longer periods at a time*. If there is no music, then *I will get antsy and want to leave at any time*. So music not only *improves my concentration*, but it also *gives me more stamina for studying* as well.

Task 2 Extended Cafeteria Hours

Reading p.72

| Analyzing |

1 Ⓒ

2 The cafeteria will be open an additional twenty-six hours (four extra hours Mon. – Sat., two extra hours Sun.).

3 The hours have changed so that students can have more time to study at the cafeteria.

4 Answers may vary.
Students might decide to have group study sessions since the cafeteria has large tables and snacks.

Listening p.73

Script & Notes 02-27

W: Look at this. The school didn't change the cafeteria's hours last semester. It must be a new thing.

M: I guess so. I'm going to find it very helpful though.

W: Why? Do you like to eat late at night?

M: Not particularly. But during finals week, my schedule is going to be a mess.

W: Do you plan on studying a lot?

M: Oh, yes. I'll have two study groups that will meet every evening. The last one finishes at 10:00 PM, which is when the library closes.

W: Gosh. So you won't have any time for dinner before that.

M: Last semester, I was starving after my group study sessions. I had to eat junk food. Now I can have some fruit or a sandwich while I study.

W: It seems that this will be better for your health.

M: And it will give me a place to continue studying

late at night. My roommate goes to bed early, so I can use the cafeteria.

W: It does have big tables, and it will probably be quiet there late at night.

M: It'll be the perfect place to do some studying before bed.

》Notes》

The man feels *happy* about the announcement.

Reason 1 *is usually hungry and has to eat junk food after studying; now can eat fruit or sandwiches after his study groups meet*

Reason 2 *can also study later because his roommate goes to bed early*

Key Words and Details *helpful, finals week, study groups, time for dinner, junk food, roommate, self-study*

Synthesizing

p.73

1   He says it will be better for his health because he won't have to eat junk food.

2   He mentions this because he says that he can study longer since the cafeteria will be open late.

3   There are big tables, and it is probably quiet late at night.

Speaking

p.74

▶ **Guided Response**   02-28

The students are discussing the announcement, which states that *the cafeteria will be extending its hours*. The change is being made because *students need a place to study late at night*. After the change, students will be able to *have some healthy snacks and a quiet place to study*. The man feels *good about the change* because he plans to *study a lot* during finals week. He says that he will *go to the cafeteria* after he meets with his study groups. This is good because he can *have some healthy food* instead of eating *junk food*. Usually, he eats *unhealthy food during finals week*. So this will be good for *his health*. His other reason is that he can *stay up late studying* in the cafeteria. His roommate *goes to bed early*, and the cafeteria is *quiet and has big tables*, which makes it a good place *to study after the library closes*.

Task 3 Life Science: Commensalism

Reading

p.75

| Analyzing |

1   Ⓓ

2   The host animal provides a benefit to another creature but is not affected at all.

3   Because even a small change to the host animal means that the relationship is not commensalism.

4   Answers may vary.
    I grew up around cows, and there are birds that stand on them.

Listening

p.76

Script & Notes 02-29

Professor: The last type of relationship I'd like to talk about today is called commensalism. You've probably not heard this word and for good reason: Parasitism and mutualism are much more common. In a commensal relationship, one organism benefits while the other is not affected.

Even though we live in the city, I'm sure most of us have driven by cattle fields. Have you ever noticed the birds that hang around the cows and sometimes even stand on the cows' backs? Those birds are called egrets, and they are a classic example of commensalism. When cattle walk around the grass in a field, underground insects come up to the top. Since egrets eat insects, it's like shooting fish in a barrel for them.

Barnacles are another animal that benefits from commensal relationships. For those who don't know, barnacles are little creatures that live in shells, sort of like crabs or lobsters. But most barnacles never leave their shells. They attach their shells to a hard surface, such as the underside of a whale or a coral reef. The creature they are attached to attracts food, and the barnacle uses its legs to bring leftovers into its shell. The host organism neither benefits nor suffers from this.

Topic *examples of commensalism*

Detail 1 *egrets stand on cows' backs and eat the bugs that the cows bring up from the ground*

Detail 2 *barnacles attach to a whale or coral reef and gather leftover food that comes near them*

Key Words *cattle fields, hang around, classic example, underground insects, shell, underside, leftovers*

Synthesizing

p.76

1   It is uncommon because any benefit or injury changes the type of relationship.

2   Egrets eat insects that come out of the ground around cows, but they do not affect the cows.

3   Barnacles attach to a hard surface and eat leftover food that comes nearby.

Speaking

p.77

▶ **Guided Response**

02-30

The professor speaks about *two relationships that demonstrate commensalism*. The first relationship, *between cows and egrets*, happens when *egrets stand on the cows' backs*. The cows move around, which makes *insects come up out of the ground*. Egrets can then *easily eat the insects as meals*. Cows, on the other hand, do not *eat insects*, and they are not *hurt by this*. The other relationship is between *barnacles and other animals such as whales*. Whales are large and broad, so barnacles *attach themselves to whales' undersides*. The host animal *brings food near the barnacles*, so the barnacles *have an easier time eating the leftovers*. These two relationships demonstrate that sometimes *two animals can get along in a way that helps one but does not affect the other*. This is different from *mutualism and parasitism* and can be hard to prove since *any effect at all means that the relationship is not commensal*.

Task 4 Zoology: Animal Desert Adaptations

Listening

p.78

Script & Notes 02-31

Professor: Deserts are harsh environments for animals to live in. Many deserts are very hot. In addition, they get very little annual precipitation. As a result, animals have to adapt to survive and thrive in deserts. Let me tell you about the adaptations which allow two very different animals to survive in deserts.

The African bullfrog is a very large frog. As you know, frogs hatch in water and spend much of their lives in aquatic environments. So what's a frog doing in the desert? Well, the African bullfrog has found a way to beat the heat and dryness. Basically, it burrows into the ground whenever the weather conditions are hot and dry. Then, it sheds its skin, which forms a cocoon around the frog. The skin prevents any moisture from leaving and can even absorb water in the ground. The frog then becomes dormant until it rains. It can do this for more than a year.

A much different animal is the desert bighorn sheep, which lives in North America. The bighorn sheep doesn't need to drink water during the summer months. The reason is that it can consume grass and obtain water from that vegetation. However, there are other times when it does need water. Well, do you see those horns? It can use its horns to open cactuses. Then, it eats the flesh of the plants, which contains water. The bighorn sheep also doesn't need to drink water for a few days. It can lose approximately one-fifth of its body weight before it needs to drink. This lets it travel long distances in search of water sources.

Topic *two animals that have adapted to life in the desert*

Detail 1 *African bullfrog = burrows into the ground in hot and dry conditions; sheds its skin; forms a cocoon; prevents moisture from leaving; can absorb water; becomes dormant until it rains*

Detail 2 *desert bighorn sheep = does not drink water in summer; gets water from eating grass; uses horns to open cactuses; can eat the watery flesh; does not need to drink water for a few days*

Key Words *burrows into the ground; sheds its skin; forms a cocoon; becomes dormant; consume grass; uses its horns to open cactuses; doesn't need to drink water*

Speaking   p.79

▶ **Guided Response**   02-32

The professor talks about *the African bullfrog and the desert bighorn sheep* and how *they have adapted to life in the desert*. She points out that the African bullfrog *has found a way to survive in hot, dry deserts*. It can *burrow into the ground and shed its skin*. The skin then *forms a cocoon which keeps moisture in* and can *collect moisture from the ground*. The bullfrog can become dormant for more than a year as it *waits until rainy weather comes*. As for the desert bighorn sheep, it doesn't need to drink water in summer because *it gets water from grass it eats*. It can also use its horns to *cut open cactuses and then eat their watery flesh*. Finally, the sheep can *survive without water for several days*. That gives it enough time to *travel to find water sources in the desert*.

◼ Chapter | 05 Independent Speaking

Task 1 Advantages and Disadvantages of Asking Questions

Brainstorming   p.82

| **Critical Thinking** |

Answers may vary.

1   I'm much more comfortable asking questions to my friends than to my teachers.

2   Teachers have a lot of knowledge and know how to explain things well, and friends know how to explain things in language you can understand.

3   Teachers are sometimes too busy to answer questions, and friends might make fun of you if you don't understand something very easy.

Organizing   p.84

Answers may vary.

> **My Choice:** *Ask friends*
>
> **Advantages:** *can explain things in language easy to understand*
>
> **Disadvantages:** *might make fun of me; might not know the answers themselves*

Speaking   p.84

▶ **Guided Response 1 Ask Friends**   02-33

There are both advantages and disadvantages to *asking friends questions when you don't understand something*. As for advantages, friends know *how to explain things in language that you understand*. I asked my friend *a math question* the other day, and *his explanation was much better than the teacher's*. I was able easily to understand it. As for the disadvantages, sometimes *friends might laugh at a person* or *make fun of that person for not knowing something*. This is especially true if *the answer to the question is very easy*. In addition, a friend might *not know the answer to the question*. My friend asked me *the answer to a history question* last week, but I didn't know the correct answer. She should have *asked the teacher instead of me*.

▶ **Guided Response 2 Ask Teachers**   02-34

I can think of both advantages and disadvantages to *asking teachers questions when I don't understand something*. First, one advantage is that *teachers have lots of knowledge*. This means they should be able to *answer your questions*. In addition, teachers *have experience explaining problems*, so they *know what to say to make students understand them*. On the other hand, there are also disadvantages. For example, *some teachers are too busy to answer questions*. They also might not *have time to give long explanations*. My science teacher always *gives short answers since she's busy*. Her answers aren't helpful. And some teachers might think *you aren't smart if you ask too many questions*. I don't want *my teachers to think I'm stupid*, so I don't always ask question in class.

Task 2 New Literature Major Requirements

Reading

p.86

| Analyzing |

1 Ⓓ

2 Students meet with an advisor who helps them choose a topic, conduct research, and write.

3 A committee reads the thesis, and the student must defend it.

4 Answers may vary.
   Literature majors could become better writers because of their theses.

Listening

p.87

Script & Notes 02-35

W: You're a Lit major, aren't you? Did you see this announcement?

M: Yeah, I got an email about it. Pretty neat, huh?

W: I thought you would be upset about it. That's going to be a lot of extra work. Writing a thesis is no joke.

M: That's true. It's going to be a lot of work. But I'm a Lit major. I hope to become a professional writer. A project like this will help me develop my skills.

W: What do you mean?

M: When you write a thesis, your advisor shows you things that you need to change. That will help me identify my weaknesses.

W: I see. So you'll grow stronger as a writer.

M: Most likely. And not only that, but think about how great this will be: one-on-one interaction with a professor.

W: It is not so common in undergraduate school.

M: Yep. I don't often get to talk directly to my professors. But with the thesis program, I'll have lots of private time to discuss things. I'll learn so much more this way than I would in a class.

W: It sounds like you've got it all worked out.

Notes

The man feels *happy* about the announcement.

Reason 1 *can help him identify his weaknesses by the advisor showing him where he needs to change*

Reason 2 *gives one-on-one interaction with a professor*

Key Words and Details *professional writer, develop my skills, grow stronger, one-on-one interaction, private time*

Synthesizing

p.87

1 He will have to write a thesis since he is a Literature major.

2 He says that he will grow as a writer by having one-on-one mentoring from a professor.

3 He thinks that it is beneficial to students and that it is uncommon in undergraduate programs.

Speaking

p.88

▶ Guided Response

02-36

The announcement states that *students who are majoring in Literature will be required to write a senior thesis before they can graduate*. After writing it, the thesis must be *defended by the student in front of a committee*. Literature students cannot graduate unless *they successfully complete this assignment*. The man reacts *positively* to the announcement. He thinks that, overall, it will *help him grow stronger as a writer*. The first reason he gives for his opinion is *that the thesis advisor can show him how to improve his writing*. He wants to become a professional writer, and the thesis will help him *identify his weaknesses*. In that way, he can improve *his chances of becoming a successful writer*. The other reason he gives is that *he will learn more because of the assignment*. He believes this is true because *he will get one-on-one interaction with a professor*. As a result, he will learn *more than by just attending class*.

Task 3 Human Biology: The Immune System

Reading
p.89

| Analyzing |

1   Ⓑ

2   The immune system keeps us healthy and has enabled humans to survive.

3   It alerts us of problems and sometimes takes direct action.

4   Answers may vary.
    The immune system alerts us through things like coughing, scratching, or sneezing.

Listening
p.90

Script & Notes 02-37

Professor: Our bodies are constantly under attack by bacteria and other microorganisms that want to live inside us. Many of these organisms are parasites, meaning that they benefit from hurting us. That's not a very good situation for us, right? And that's why our bodies have developed an immune system. It keeps us healthy—or tries anyway.

One way that the immune system works is with white blood cells. These cells attack bacteria that enter our bodies. They quickly reproduce when there is a problem. Then, they travel to the area where the invading bacteria are. You can easily tell when this is happening. You'll see a red spot on your skin. The area may even swell up. The reason is that the blood is concentrating in one area to fight the bacteria.

The immune system has another trick. Instead of fighting invaders, it tries to kick them right out. You've probably guessed by now what I'm talking about, which is sneezing. Maybe you've wondered why we sneeze. Now you know. It's your body's way of expelling harmful microorganisms.

Notes

Topic *ways the immune system protects our bodies*

Detail 1 *white blood cells are produced when bacteria enter our bodies*
illustrated by red spots on skin or swelling

Detail 2 *The body may try to kick out the invaders.*
illustrated by sneezing

Key Words *parasites, white blood cells, invading bacteria, red spot, swell up, kick them out, harmful microorganisms*

Synthesizing
p.90

1   The professor explains two ways that the immune system works.

2   She talks about red spots and swelling on the skin and about sneezing.

3   Visual changes, such as red spots and swelling, demonstrate alerts.

Speaking
p.91

▶ Guided Response   02-38

The professor begins with a brief introduction to *the topic of the immune system*. As explained in the reading, the immune system is *a network of cells, tissues, and organs* that protect the body from *harmful bacteria*. The professor mentions that bacteria are *parasites*, so the body wants to *take care of them quickly*. She clarifies the topic by giving *two examples of how the immune system works*. The first example, *white blood cells*, demonstrates how the body *immediately attacks invading bacteria*. The immune system produces *white blood cells*, which *rush to the area of infection*. We can observe this happening when *we see a red spot on our skin*. The second example, *sneezing*, shows that the immune system may attempt to *kick out the bacteria instead of attacking them*. When the immune system *detects a threat*, it may *trigger a sneeze*, which will hopefully *expel the bacteria from the body*.

Task 4 Animal Science: Cooperative Hunting

Listening   p.92

Script & Notes 02-39

Professor: In the never-ending search for food, animals have evolved a great number of strategies. Many creatures hunt for food. While some species hunt alone, others have found success by hunting in groups. They sometimes even hunt alongside animals of another species.

The most basic and easiest-to-observe cooperative hunting technique is pack hunting. Wild dogs have become experts at pack hunting. They gather together in a group of at least nine dogs and search for prey. They roam the fields until they find a group of prey. When the prey animals realize the danger, they run away. The wild dogs chase the slowest prey animal and work together to take it down. Pack hunting is advantageous because it allows the takedown of larger animals. On its own, a wild dog could only take down small prey, which usually runs faster than large prey. Large prey animals are slower, but a lone dog cannot take one down.

Another type of cooperative hunting involves different species working together to increase their hunting success. We call it complementary hunting because two species with different hunting styles work together to catch prey. The ocean offers an interesting example of this. Two species—the grouper fish and the moray eel—cooperate to catch food. Groupers hunt in the open waters while moray eels hide between rocks and coral reefs. A grouper working with a moray eel may chase its prey into the eel's hiding place, where the eel catches its next meal. Likewise, an eel may scare its prey out of the rocks and into the open water, where the predatory grouper is waiting with its mouth open.

Notes

Topic *cooperative hunting = animals working together to hunt*

Detail 1 *pack hunting = animals of the same species hunting together*

ex: wild dogs work together in groups to take down larger prey

Detail 2 *complementary hunting = different species hunting together*

ex: grouper fish and moray eel – each animal scares prey toward the other in a rock or in the open water

Key Words *technique, at least nine dogs, group of prey, larger animals, different hunting styles, open waters, hide*

Speaking   p.93

▶ **Guided Response**   02-40

The professor is explaining *cooperative hunting*. Put simply, this is when *two or more animals work together to hunt*. There are two basic types of *cooperative hunting*. The first is *pack hunting*. The professor explains it by *talking about groups of wild dogs*. Whenever wild dogs *go out in search of prey*, they *travel in groups of nine or more*. This provides them with benefits because *they are able to take down much larger prey than they could alone*. So cooperative hunting improves *the wild dogs' chances of survival*. The second type is *called complementary hunting*. This is when two animals of *different species and hunting styles work together*. The professor discusses *the grouper fish and the moray eel* to demonstrate this kind of hunting. The grouper fish *chases prey in the open water toward the moray eel, which is hiding in rocks or coral reefs*. Other times, the moray eel *scares prey out into the open water, where the grouper fish is waiting*. Both animals benefit because *they have greater hunting success*.

◗ Chapter | 06 Independent Speaking

Task 1 University: Hometown vs. Out of Town

Brainstorming   p.96

| Critical Thinking |

Answers may vary.

1   It can be difficult because you don't have any

friends and don't know the area.

2   Staying in my hometown means I can be near my friends and family and feel more comfortable.

3   Going away would help me grow as a person and challenge myself while staying at home would probably let me focus more on my studies.

Organizing

p.98

Answers may vary.

> **My Choice:** *stay in hometown*
>
> **Reason 1:** *save time and money by staying with parents – not waste time on laundry or cooking*
>
> **Reason 2:** *have social network already – not have to meet new people*

Speaking

p.98

▶ **Guided Response 1 Hometown**   02-41

When I go to university, I would like to *stay in my hometown*. While moving away may be adventurous, I think staying home *would better allow me to achieve my goals*. As a practical person, staying in my hometown would allow me to *stay with my parents and save time and money*. Because I would not have to *do laundry or cook meals*, I would have more *free time to do other things*. For example, I could *spend more time studying*. In addition to that, moving away would *give me extra stress from loneliness*. That stress does not *exist whenever I am in my hometown*. I can *spend time with my friends and family* and not worry about *trying to go out and meet new people*. That way, I could focus more on *my studies*.

▶ **Guided Response 2 Another City**   02-42

I believe that *going to another city* would *be the better choice for me*. Therefore, I would not stay *in my hometown*. I know someone who stayed *in our hometown for university*. I noticed that she *did not change at all as a person*. This leads me to think that moving away *is a challenge that tests your strengths and weaknesses*. This would help me to grow as a person because *I would need to adapt to the new city and living environment*. Besides that, moving away would give me the opportunity to *meet lots of new people*. One of my goals in university will be *to create a larger social network*. If I stay at home, I cannot *do this* because *everyone knows me and I already have a reputation*.

Task 2 Healthy Food Options

Reading

p.100

| Analyzing |

1   (A)

2   She considers herself someone who is concerned with being healthy.

3   They are examples of some of the foods that the student would like to see in the convenience stores.

4   Answers may vary.
    Some students may prefer to eat hotdogs or candy bars to fruit and salad.

Listening

p.101

Script & Notes 02-43

W: I couldn't agree more about this letter. Have you ever been in the convenience stores on campus? They have nothing but junk food.

M: True, but you don't have to eat there. The cafeteria serves healthy meals every day.

W: But I don't always have time to go to the cafeteria. I only have a one-hour break between classes.

M: That's enough time to go to the cafeteria.

W: Yes, but I'd rather spend that time studying. I only have time to grab a snack from the store.

M: You make a good point. People need quick options because of their busy schedules.

W: Besides that, look at the example it sets. The university is promoting junk food to students. What kind of message does that send?

M: That the university doesn't believe in healthy eating.

W: Exactly. These days, everyone knows how important your diet is. I expect the university to promote responsible eating.

M: And hotdogs and candy bars are hardly healthy. I think you're right. The university should provide healthier options.

The woman *agrees* with the letter.

Reason 1 *does not have much time between classes and wants to study instead of using her time to go to the cafeteria*

Reason 2 *selling junk food sets a bad example for students and encourages unhealthy diets*

Key Words and Details *junk food, busy schedule, one-hour break, quick options, busy schedule, message, responsible eating*

Synthesizing
p.101

1   She personalizes the ideas by saying how the junk food selection affects her negatively.

2   She can't go to the cafeteria because she would rather use her free time to study.

3   Part of a university's role is to encourage students to eat healthy foods.

Speaking
p.102

▶ **Guided Response**
02-44

The woman expresses her opinion about *a letter to the school newspaper*. In the letter, a student says *that the campus convenience stores should offer healthier food choices*. The current options on campus are *mostly junk food, such as hotdogs and candy bars*. The woman *agrees* with this for two reasons. First, she says that *she would like to have healthier snacks between classes*. She explains that her schedule *only allows one-hour breaks*. Therefore, she does not have time *to go to the cafeteria for a healthy meal*. Second, she explains that a university *needs to promote healthy eating to its students*. The food options available now promote *unhealthy diets*, which the woman thinks *is irresponsible*. By selling healthier options, *she would have a better selection of foods to eat between classes, and students would be encouraged to eat healthy foods*. Therefore, she thinks the letter *delivers a message she can agree with*.

Task 3 Zoology: Pack Behavior

Reading
p.103

| Analyzing |

1   Ⓓ

2   They live, migrate, hunt, and eat together.

3   The leader is the alpha male or female, higher-ranking animals are betas, and the lowest animal is the omega.

4   Answers may vary.
Animals can get security by being in a pack, and they can also get more access to food.

Listening
p.104

Script & Notes 02-45

Professor: I'm sure everyone knows wolves live in packs. As a general rule, the wolves in a pack are related. They're led by an alpha male, whose mate is usually the alpha female. Why do wolves live in packs? There are a couple of reasons for this behavior.

First, wolves can hunt much better when they are in a pack. Sure, a lone wolf can kill a rabbit or squirrel and have a meal. But after some time, there won't be many small animals left. Instead, wolves prefer to hunt larger animals such as deer and elk. It's difficult for a wolf to take down one of these large animals by itself. But by hunting in a pack, wolves can kill large animals and gain access to a large amount of meat. The meat can feed an entire pack for several days in many cases.

Second, the pack can provide protection for its members. Very few animals will challenge a wolf pack in its own territory. However, if one wolf is off by itself, it could be killed by other wolves or by a bear or other animal. In that way, living in a pack help keeps wolves alive.

Topic *how packs benefit wolves*

Detail 1 *can hunt much better in a pack*

can hunt large animals; deer and elk; cannot take down alone; gain access to large amount of meat; feed for days

Detail 2 *provide protection for members*

few animals will challenge wolf pack; can be killed alone; living in packs keeps wolves alive

Key Words *hunt much better; hunt larger animals; feed an entire pack; provide protection; keeps wolves alive*

Synthesizing
p.104

1 The professor discusses how wolves hunt together and get protection by staying together. Both of these activities show pack behavior.

2 The professor states that lone wolves can only kill small animals and may also be killed by other predators.

3 Wolves can gain access to larger amounts of food and be protected by the other members of their pack.

Speaking
p.105

▶ **Guided Response**
02-46

The professor lectures to the students *about wolves*. He points out that wolves often *live together in groups called packs*. There are two main benefits to *living in packs*. First, lone wolves *can only kill small animals such as rabbits and squirrels*. However, wolves in packs *can hunt together and kill large animals such as deer and elk*. Those kills can give wolves *very much food that lasts for several days*. Second, wolves can be *protected better by being in a pack*. Lone wolves may *get killed by bears or other predators*, but few animals will *challenge a pack in its territory*. The actions of wolves are related to *pack behavior*. Pack behavior describes *how animals such as wolves and dogs live, migrate, hunt, and eat together*. Each animal in a pack, including *the alpha male, the alpha female, the betas, and the omega*, has its behavior determined *by its social standing in the pack*.

Task 4 Business: Targeted Marketing

Listening
p.106

Script & Notes 02-47

Professor: When you get out of college and start being involved in marketing projects, you're going to have to make a lot of decisions. One of the first things you'll need to decide is whether or not to use targeted marketing to sell your product or service.

Targeted marketing is a strategy that, just like it sounds, targets specific segments of the population. Once you identify who is probably going to buy your product, you direct your advertising to those people. The clearest way to see targeted marketing is in magazines. Open a magazine for women, and you'll find ads for cleaning products, children's toys, and other things that are usually purchased by women. If you open a men's magazine, you're going to find ads for things like cologne and sports equipment. You probably won't see an advertisement for paper towels in a men's magazine. The reason is that research shows that women overwhelmingly do the household shopping.

This type of marketing works great if your product is only going to be purchased by some groups of the population. It won't work for everything though. Let's say you're advertising a cruise trip. Everyone likes to go on trips, so you would not want to limit your marketing to one group. Doing so would cut off potential customers. Instead, you would try to reach as many groups as possible with a general marketing plan. How do you accomplish this? Comedy programs, billboards, newspapers . . . These are things that people from all walks of life will come across, so you are trying to reach as many customers as your marketing budget will allow.

Topic *examples of when to use targeted marketing*

Detail 1 *marketing that targets specific groups of people who will buy your product*

ex: women's magazine ads, such as cleaning products and children's toys

Detail 2 *not good for products with general interest*

ex: cruise trips, which everyone enjoys

Key Words *specific segments, direct advertising, children's toys, cologne or sports equipment, purchased by some groups, reach as many groups as possible*

Speaking p.107

▶ **Guided Response** 02-48

The topic of the lecture is *targeted marketing*. The professor briefly defines this as *using a marketing plan that targets specific segments of society*. To illustrate the concept, the professor first gives examples of *men's and women's magazines*. He explains that in *women's magazines*, you'll find advertisements for things like *cleaning products and children's toys*. In *men's magazines*, you'll see advertisements for *sports equipment* but not for paper towels. The reason is that *men and women tend to buy different products*, so the advertising is *targeted at either of them*. The last part of the lecture talks about *when to use targeted marketing*. For some products, targeted marketing *is not good because people from all walks of life may want to buy the product*. This is illustrated with the example of *a cruise trip*. Since all kinds of people *want to go on luxury vacations*, you should advertise in *newspapers or on billboards, which are things that many different people are likely to see*.

▶ Chapter | **07** Independent Speaking

Task 1 Overpaid Entertainers

Brainstorming p.110

| **Critical Thinking** |

Answers may vary.

1   I think they earn high salaries because millions of people pay to watch them or to listen to them.

2   Almost no one earns as much as entertainers do.

---

3   People who provide the most benefit and work the hardest deserve the highest salaries.

Organizing p.112

Answers may vary.

My Choice: *disagree*

Reason 1: *high stress job – perform for demanding audiences even if feel bad*

Reason 2: *provide important function in society: entertainment*

Speaking p.112

▶ **Guided Response 1 Agree** 02-49

It is clear that entertainers *are overpaid*. They earn far more *money than they deserve*. Their salaries are too high. I believe that a salary should be determined by *the difficulty of a position or the training it requires*. Entertainers do not *have very difficult jobs to do*, so they should not *earn such high salaries*. Other professions, such as *doctors, who must study for many years and work under great stress, should earn* more money. Another reason is that *their high salaries turn entertainers into role models*. When I see entertainers, I notice that *they often act badly, like fighting in public*. If entertainers did not earn such high salaries, *young people would not admire them or their bad behavior*. I think everyone would agree that *entertainers are overpaid*.

▶ **Guided Response 2 Disagree** 02-50

I am of the belief that *entertainers are not overpaid*. I think that entertainers work *harder than most people realize*. Many people think it is a *luxurious and relaxing* lifestyle, but *celebrities actually have a lot of stress*. They must deal with *difficult audiences wanting to be entertained even if they are in a bad mood or sick*. This makes their jobs difficult, so *I think they deserve to be paid well for it*. I would also argue that entertainers are *important to society*. They provide society with *entertainment, which everyone wants*. This is valuable to society because *we all need a way to relax, and entertainment helps us do that*. Because of their importance to society, *celebrities deserve to be paid high salaries*. That's why I think *entertainers aren't overpaid*.

Task 2 Boat Rentals

Reading
p.114

| Analyzing |

1 Ⓑ

2 She provides one reason why the school should lower the price to support her opinion.

3 The student argues that the rental fee is too high for most students to afford to use a boat.

4 Answers may vary.
More students could rent boats and then learn how to sail on a boat.

Listening
p.115

Script & Notes 02-51

M: Huh, I didn't even know you could rent boats at Bear Lake now. I'm glad the school is doing that.

W: It's pretty new. I think the boats just arrived a week ago. Are you thinking of going sailing on the lake sometime soon?

M: It's definitely an activity that I would like to try. I've always wanted to learn how to sail a boat. I think it would be rather exciting.

W: Yeah, but what do you think about the information in this letter? I mean, 20 dollars is pretty expensive.

M: You know, I have mixed feelings about this. On the one hand, you're right. Paying that much money is not possible for lots of students. I can afford to do it once or twice, but I can't make a habit of it.

W: I'm the same way.

M: On the other hand, those boats aren't cheap.

W: What do you mean?

M: The school surely spent a lot of money on those boats. Maintaining them isn't cheap either. The school needs to recover the money it invested in the boats. So I also understand why the rental fee is so high.

W: Yeah, that makes sense. I hadn't really looked at it that way.

Notes

The man has *mixed feelings* about the letter.

Reason 1 *not possible for many students to pay the rental fee; could do it once or twice; can't make a habit of it*

Reason 2 *school spent lots of money on boats; needs to recover its investment; understands why the fee is high*

Key Words and Details *mixed feelings; could afford to do it once or twice; boats aren't cheap; maintaining them; recover the money it invested*

Synthesizing
p.115

1 The man states that he has mixed feelings about the information in the letter.

2 He states that the minimum amount of money required to rent a boat is too high for most students.

3 He says that the school needs to recover the money that it invested in the boats.

Speaking
p.116

▶ Guided Response
02-52

The man and the woman are talking about *a letter to the editor about boat rentals at Bear Lake*. The man states that *he has mixed feelings* about the remarks made by the writer of the letter. First of all, he comments that he agrees that *the minimum rental fee is too high*. He points out that *many students cannot afford to pay that much money*. About himself, he notes that he *could pay it a couple of times* but *could not make a habit of renting a boat*. However, the man also *understands why the fee is so high*. He says that the school *spent a lot of money on the boats* and *needs to pay money to maintain them*. Because the school has to *recover its investment in the boats*, he thinks that *the high price of renting them is acceptable*.

Task 3 Psychology: Sensory Memory

Reading

p.117

| Analyzing |

1　Ⓐ

2　It needed a new name because it is much shorter than even short-term memory.

3　They are visual information automatically stored in the brain.

4　Answers may vary.
　　It would remember things that we see briefly, such as advertisements.

Listening

p.118

Script & Notes 02-53

Professor: Today, we are going to talk about sensory memory, which is the brain's ability to momentarily store memories. Every time you hear or see something, the brain remembers it. If you do not make use of the information, your brain forgets it. All of this happens on the subconscious level, meaning that you don't always know that it's happening. That's why it's called sensory memory—because your senses do all the work.

　　A landmark study on sensory memory was done by Dr. George Sperling in 1960. In his study, he made a grid of three rows of four letters in each. The grid was flashed in front of participants' eyes for less than half a second. He then asked them to recall as many letters as they could. Most participants recalled about four letters. When he repeated the experiment, he asked participants to remember letters only from one row. Participants usually recalled the entire row, but no more. This proved that, for about a second or two after seeing the grid, participants had a "photograph" of the grid in their minds. That photograph is what we call sensory memory.

Notes

Topic *a kind of memory that is automatically stored and doesn't last long*

Detail 1 *happens subconsciously: if you do not think about the memories, then they go away*

Detail 2 *a study showed a grid of letters to subjects for half a second; showed that people take a quick "photograph"*

Key Words *subconscious level, senses, half a second, four letters, row, photograph*

Synthesizing

p.118

1　They are often not recognized consciously, and they are quickly forgotten.

2　The study asked participants to recall letters from a grid. They almost always remembered three or four letters.

3　The professor makes the comparison because the memories are like images rather than concrete memories.

Speaking

p.119

▶ **Guided Response** 02-54

Sensory memory is a kind of memory that *is shorter than short-term and long-term memory*. It happens in the *senses*, and sometimes we don't *know it is happening*. These memories do not *last very long*. According to the reading, they last *only a second or two*. The professor further explains this idea by *describing a study that was done*. In the study, participants saw *some letters of the alphabet on a grid*. They *only saw the grid for about half a second*, and then they were asked to *recall the letters*. The experiment showed that participants usually could *remember four letters anywhere on the grid*, or they could *recall four letters in a single row*. Either way, they typically only *recalled three or four letters*. This showed that *the eyes take a photograph of everything they see*. If we think quickly, we can *recall some details of things that we have just seen*. That is called *sensory memory*.

Task 4 History: Sun Tzu

Listening
p.120

Script & Notes 02-55

Professor: Today, I'd like to talk about one of the great leaders in military history: Sun Tzu. He was a Chinese military leader best known for *The Art of War*, a series of documents he wrote about military strategy. Sun Tzu lived at a time of constant war in China, some twenty-five hundred years ago. His teachings influenced fighting in his time as well as future wars.

During Sun Tzu's own lifetime, he was an advisor to a ruling lord in China. He taught the ruler to understand his enemy's strengths and weaknesses. Using his strategies, the ruler became victorious. Sun Tzu's teachings spread, and generals began to use his strategies. Within two hundred years, the entire concept of war in China had changed. Wars in China became less traditional and more brutal. Leaders began to take advantage of enemy weaknesses and focused on winning.

Even in more modern times, military leaders have looked to Sun Tzu for knowledge. Napoleon Bonaparte was well known as a student of Sun Tzu. He used Sun Tzu's strategies to great success until he finally ignored the Chinese general's teachings, which led to a major defeat in Russia. You see, he ignored Sun Tzu's instructions to consider the land. In Russia, there was not enough agriculture to support France's army. Napoleon continued into Russia anyway, and his army did not have enough food. His soldiers became weak from starvation and disease, so Napoleon lost to Russia.

Notes

Topic *Chinese military advisor Sun Tzu influenced ancient Chinese war and future wars*

Detail 1 *taught generals to take advantage of the enemy's weaknesses*

China's wars changed from more traditional to brutal and focused on winning

Detail 2 *Napoleon Bonaparte = student of Sun Tzu*

Ignored Sun Tzu's teaching (pay attention to land) and his soldiers starved – lost war in Russia

Key Words *military strategy, ruling lord, strategies, concept of war, take advantage, weakness, major defeat, Russia, starvation*

Speaking
p.121

▶ **Guided Response**
02-56

The professor is describing a historical figure, *Sun Tzu*, who was *a military leader in ancient China*. Sun Tzu wrote about *military strategy*, and his teachings became popular. Using examples from *ancient and modern times*, the professor shows *the influence Sun Tzu has had*. In ancient China, fighting was *changed by Sun Tzu's teachings*. He said that you should *learn about your enemies and find out where they are strong or weak*. Soon after people began studying his strategies, Chinese wars *became more severe*. The rulers concentrated on *winning more than anything else*. The professor explains that *Sun Tzu's teachings* were an influence on Napoleon as well. Napoleon studied Sun Tzu and had success by *following Sun Tzu's teachings*. However, he did not *obey Sun Tzu's advice in the war against Russia*. His soldiers *died from starvation and disease* because *Napoleon pushed them into land with no food*. This ignored Sun Tzu's teachings to *know the land*.

Chapter | 08 Independent Speaking

Task 1 Experienced Teacher vs. New Teacher

Brainstorming
p.124

| **Critical Thinking** |
Answers may vary.

1   If I am happy, I learn better, but if I am bored or upset, I cannot learn well.

2 A teacher's life experience and personal knowledge is probably more important than the textbook.

3 I think it is a skill that is learned through practice, like with any profession.

Task 2 Eating in Class

Organizing
p.126

Answers may vary.

> **My Choice:** *experienced teacher*
>
> **Reason 1:** *will know more about the subject*
>
> **Reason 2:** *will have effective teaching methods*

Reading
p.128

| Analyzing |

1 Ⓒ

2 The decision was made by the student council after great discussion.

3 The goal is to increase student concentration and to allow end-of-semester parties.

4 Answers may vary.
   Students will probably begin eating in class, and I think they will make a mess.

Speaking
p.126

▶ **Guided Response 1 Experienced Teacher** 02-57

Given this choice, I would prefer *to have a teacher who is experienced but unenthusiastic*. Even though a teacher may be boring, he or she *will know a good deal about the topic*. This is more useful to me as a student because *a teacher's insight can increase my understanding*. For example, one of my teachers *has been a professional writer for twenty years*. He is not very fun, but he *can teach us so much about language usage*. Because of this, the students *have really improved as writers*. Another reason is that an experienced teacher knows *the best teaching methods*. This means that the teacher can *effectively deliver the important information*. In a nutshell, I think that an experienced teacher *has more to teach* and *is better at teaching*.

▶ **Guided Response 2 New Teacher** 02-58

As a student, I always prefer a teacher who *is young and excited about teaching*. Even though the teacher is new, he or she can *still be an effective teacher*. There are a couple of reasons why *I feel this way*. The main reason is that an enthusiastic teacher *can motivate students to learn*. This is very important because *students who are motivated and excited will learn more*. So the teacher's enthusiasm will automatically improve the *students' performances*. In addition, a new teacher is more likely to *have innovative methods and ideas for teaching*. I find this useful because *the old ways of teaching are not always the best*. In sum, I think a new, enthusiastic teacher *can motivate the students and use fresh, exciting teaching methods*.

Listening
p.129

Script & Notes 02-59

W: Hey, we can finally bring snacks to class. That's great! I'm always hungry, which makes it really hard to concentrate.

M: I guess you're right, but I can't say I'm crazy about the change.

W: Do you mean you don't want to eat in class?

M: I mean, yes, it's great that you can concentrate better. But what about everyone else?

W: I'm not following you.

M: While you're enjoying a snack, I have to listen to you opening food containers and chewing your food. It would be quite a distraction if I'm trying to concentrate on the lecture.

W: Well, I suppose that is a possibility. Some people make a lot of noise when they eat. But what about the class parties? Those should be fun, right?

M: I guess they would be fun, but are they the best use of our time? I like to relax and have snacks, but I can do that at home.

W: But the point is to celebrate with your classmates.

M: Sure, but it seems like a waste of time to me. If the professor doesn't have a lecture, I could use that extra class time to study for my final exams.

The man *is not happy* about the announcement.

Reason 1 *other students eating in class can be a distraction because of the noise involved in eating*

Reason 2 *class time should be used for learning; students can relax or have snacks at home*

Key Words and Details *concentrate, food containers, chew food, distraction, class parties, waste of time*

Synthesizing
p.129

1   He thinks it will help the student who is eating but will be a distraction for everyone else.

2   He is worried that he won't be able to concentrate on the lectures if the other students around him are eating.

3   He likes to relax and have fun, but he would rather spend that time studying for his final exams.

Speaking
p.130

▶ **Guided Response**   02-60

The man is explaining why *he opposes the information in the announcement*, which declares that *food is no longer banned in classrooms*. The announcement states that *professors can choose to allow students to eat food in class* so that they can *concentrate better on full stomachs* and *have parties to celebrate the end of a semester*. The man *is strongly opposed to* this rule change. The first reason the man *is against it* is that he thinks *the food would be a distraction*. He says that *people chew loudly on their food and loudly open wrappers*. This would *cause a distraction for him during a lecture when he is trying to concentrate*. Furthermore, he states that *he is not interested in end-of-the-semester parties*. He feels that *the only reason to go to class is to learn*. Instead of having a party, he would rather *study for a final exam or relax at home*.

Task 3 Business: Aggressive Marketing

Reading
p.131

| Analyzing |

1   Ⓑ

2   Companies that need aggressive marketing are those that have a lot of competition.

3   The goal is for a company to make itself be noticed by consumers.

4   Answers may vary.
    Aggressive marketing probably bothers people more than basic advertising does.

Listening
p.132

Script & Notes 02-61

Professor: Have you ever been at home and gotten a phone call from a marketing company? Someone calls you out of the blue and tries to talk you into buying something, right? Well, these companies are using aggressive marketing. The word aggressive means to be bold and energetic. When you practice aggressive marketing, you don't wait for consumers to find you; you find them.

I'll tell you how this works in the real world. These days, health and fitness clubs are extremely popular. It seems that a new one opens here every week. If you look around, you'll see that they are all basically the same, too. How can a health club convince people to join? Let's say that a new health club opens and that it wants to be the best in the area. It starts by mailing special-offer coupons to everyone who lives nearby. Maybe the coupon offers a 50% discount on membership for the first month. People are enticed by this offer, so they decide to go to the club. After the first month, not everyone will become full members, but many will. So you can see how this would be a lot more effective than simply posting advertisements about the health club.

Notes

Topic *how businesses can use aggressive marketing to increase sales*

Detail 1 *example of a health club that wants to convince people to join*

Detail 2 *health club sends out discount coupons to attract new members*

Key Words *bold and energetic, consumers, new one every week, special offer, membership discount, enticed*

Synthesizing

p.132

1   She mentions health clubs because there are many of them and they are all similar.

2   Printing a coupon and mailing it to people who live nearby are aggressive marketing techniques.

3   The health club will entice people to become full members.

Speaking

p.133

▶ **Guided Response**

02-62

According to the passage, aggressive marketing means *to seek customers with marketing*. It is especially useful when *there is a lot of competition*. The professor explains that *marketing aggressively* can lead to *the success of a business*. She uses the example of *health and fitness clubs*. Because there are many *health clubs* and they are all *similar to one another*, it can be difficult to *attract members*. The professor explains that a new health club needs to *market aggressively in order to get members*. The example she uses is *giving away special-offer coupons*. The coupons *are mailed to people's homes*, and they offer *fifty-percent discounts for one month*. Some people will *join for the month and then quit*, but others will become *full-time members*. Because of *its aggressive marketing*, the health club now *has an advantage over health clubs that used basic advertising*.

Task 4 Animal Science: Venom

Listening

p.134

Script & Notes 02-63

Professor: One of the most remarkable physical traits that some animals have evolved is venom. This is a kind of toxin that attacks the nerves of another animal. Strong venom can completely stop an animal from moving. Venom is usually delivered into an animal by a stinger or with teeth. You can observe animals using it either for self-defense or to take down prey.

As you all know, bees have stingers. Bees will stab you if they sense that you are dangerous. No one likes a bee sting. It certainly is irritating, but it will usually not cause serious damage. The reason is mainly that humans are so much larger than bees. On the other hand, imagine that you're a bird and a bee stings you. Birds have much smaller bodies than humans do. If the bird is stung, the bee's venom will cause some of its muscles to stop working. This can put the bird in serious danger as it may not be able to fly. So you can see that the venom is quite a good deterrent. As a result, most predators will not attack bees since they don't want to get stung.

Among the snakes in the world, very many of them use venom to catch their food. A snake that uses venom injects it into its prey with its sharp teeth, called fangs. The venom works rather quickly. Once a small animal, such as a mouse, is bitten by a snake, it stands no chance of survival. The mouse will lose control of its body so that it can do nothing to defend itself while the snake swallows it whole.

Notes

Topic *venom = substance used by animals for self-defense and offense*

Detail 1 *bees use venom for self-defense against birds and other predators*

when it is stung, the bird's muscles stop working

Detail 2 *snakes use venom to kill their prey*

prey loses control of its body and can't defend itself

Key Words *physical trait, evolve, stinger, muscles, stop working, deterrent, stands no chance, lose control*

Speaking

p.135

▶ **Guided Response** 02-64

In the lecture, the professor explains *how animals use venom for self-defense and for attacking prey*. Venom is *a kind of poison that attacks an animal's nerves*. It makes the muscles *stop working*, so the animal *cannot move*. The professor gives two examples that illustrate *each way that venom is used*. He starts by speaking about bees. Bees have *stingers with venom*. When they are threatened, they *sting their target*. This can be *deadly to a small animal* such as a *bird*. Therefore, many animals avoid *bees because they do not want to be stung*. Snakes show how venom is used to *attack prey*. Venomous snakes bite *small animals with their fangs*. This delivers the venom to the animals' bodies and *locks their muscles*. The venom acts quickly, so the animals *have no way to defend themselves*. Thanks to the venom, snakes can *eat their prey without too much of a struggle*.

Part C

Actual Test | 01 p.138

Task 1

◆ **Sample Response**

Personally, I like reading about positive events more than news about negative events. To begin with, positive news stories can be inspiring. For example, yesterday, I read about a teenager who had cancer as a boy. Doctors said he probably wouldn't live long, but the boy didn't give up. He kept fighting, and he managed to defeat cancer. Today, he's going to graduate from high school and attend a top university. Stories like that inspire me. In addition, positive new stories help me feel better. There are so many bad things happening in the world nowadays that I feel much better after reading something positive. A story such as one about a firefighter saving a family from a burning home makes me feel happy. I wish there were more positive news stories to read.

Task 2

Listening

Script 03-03

W: Did you see that ridiculous letter in the school paper? Why would anybody want to reduce the number of parking spaces available on campus?

M: Actually, I thought the writer brought up a good point.

W: Really?

M: Sure. Turning that old parking lot into a small park is a great idea.

W: Do you care to explain why?

M: Well, first of all, like the letter said, there aren't many green spaces on campus. I mean, we would all benefit from having more places to go and relax between classes. And the student center is near the middle of campus, so it would be easy for all students to access.

W: I suppose you are right about that, but what about the drivers? How is this good for them?

M: You know, a lot of people drive through that parking lot to avoid the intersection on the corner. They really disrupt the flow of traffic by doing that.

W: That's true. I notice that street is always crowded with cars.

M: Right. So if the parking lot becomes a green space, traffic conditions on campus will actually improve.

◆ Sample Response

The letter to the school paper states that the school should turn an unused parking lot into a green space for students. The writer feels that turning the parking lot into a park would improve the campus environment. The man supports the writer's opinion. First, he asserts that there are not enough green spaces around the school for students. He says that all students would benefit from having a place to relax between classes. He also contends that all students could get to the park easily because it is near the student center in the middle of the campus. Furthermore, the man argues that the parking lot disrupts the flow of traffic around campus. The reason is that people drive through the parking lot to avoid the intersection. He concludes that turning the parking lot into a green space would make traffic conditions on campus better.

Task 3

Listening

Script 03-04

Professor: The expectations that scientists and participants have in an experiment can significantly affect the outcome. In these cases, the expectancy effect can be classified into two types. One is called observer expectancy, and the other is called subject expectancy. Allow me to go into detail.

In observer expectancy, the expectations of the researchers conducting an experiment can affect the results. To give a common example, let's talk about scientists studying a drug that improves athletic performance. There are two participant groups: One takes the drug, and the other takes a sugar pill. The scientists know which group got the drug, so they expect a better performance from this group. They may believe the members of this group are performing better even if they are not. As you can see, the results of the experiment become inaccurate.

As you can probably guess, subject expectancy occurs when participants have certain expectations about a situation. For instance, a woman with a headache goes to the doctor to get some treatment. The doctor examines her and determines the cause of her illness. The woman receives medicine from the doctor. After taking the first pill, her headache immediately disappears. The reason is that the woman expected the treatment to work, so it did.

◆ Sample Response

The reading passage deals with the expectancy effect. This occurs when the participants or scientists running a human behavior test know what results to expect. The expectancy effect can result in inaccurate findings being reported. In her lecture, the professor gives two examples to explain the expectancy effect in greater detail. She begins by mentioning observer expectancy, which is when the expectations of scientists affect test results. To illustrate this point, the professor describes a study of a drug that improves athletic performance. She states that scientists expect participants who take the real drug to perform better even if they actually do not. Next, the instructor discusses subject expectancy. This is a situation where participants have certain expectations about a result. She describes a woman visiting a doctor to treat a headache. The doctor examines the woman and gives her some medicine. She takes the medicine and feels better. The medicine worked because the woman expected it to work.

Task 4

Listening

Script 03-05

Professor: Pheromones are chemicals used by certain plants and animals for communication with other members of their species. Basically, one creature emits, or gives off, pheromones. Then the other members of its community sense these pheromones and react in a specific way.

Pheromones are often used to help members of a group find food. These are referred to as trail pheromones. Social creatures, such as ants, make great use of trail pheromones. Here's how they do it. First, one ant finds a source of food. This ant then travels back to the nest with some food. As it does so, it lays down pheromones that attract other ants. These ants use this scent to move between the food and their colony. Each time an ant moves along the path, the pheromone trail gets renewed. The trail continues to be renewed until the food source runs out. When that happens, the pheromone trail completely disappears.

Animals use pheromones in other ways, too. Some animals do not like sharing land with other members of their species. So these animals use territorial pheromones to—you guessed it—mark their territory. The animals lay down their scent to let other members of their species know that they are there. Two of our closest furry friends—dogs and cats—often use territorial pheromones to keep other members of their species away. This is what my cat

Sadie does. Whenever I let her outside, she sprays a scent in places around the yard. When she does this, other cats that come near will notice her scent and keep out of her territory.

◆ **Sample Response**

The topic of the lecture is pheromones, which are chemicals certain plants and animals use to cause a reaction in other members of their species. The professor talks about two different types of pheromones and the effects they have. One type is called trail pheromones. They are used by ants and other social creatures to help other members of their group find food. The professor explains that an ant that finds food leaves a trail of pheromones between the food and the ant colony. This allows other ants to find the food and to bring it back to the colony. The second type of pheromones described by the instructor is territorial pheromones. These are used by animals that do not like sharing land with other members of their species, such as dogs and cats. The lecturer describes how his own cat sprays scents around her yard. His cat does this to stop other cats from entering her territory.

Actual Test | **02**   p.146

Task 1

◆ **Sample Response**

I support the idea that it is better to review class notes regularly rather than just before exams. The first reason is that studying regularly allows learners to get better grades. Students who study throughout the semester are able to understand their learning material more deeply. They can also get help from their professors when they do not understand something. This makes them more likely to get higher scores when test time rolls around. On top of this, studying regularly allows students to retain information over the long term. When students cram the night before a test, they usually remember what they study only long enough to answer the test questions. Students who study regularly are able to remember what they learn long after the test and into adulthood.

Task 2

Listening

Script 03-08

M: Did you see this? The school is planning to extend

the hours of operation of the cafeteria in Wilson Hall. I wonder why that decision was made. It seems kind of pointless to me.

W: On the contrary, I think it's a great idea. You know, I have afternoon classes, and then I go to my part-time job in the evening. By the time I finish work, the dining halls are closed. Now, I'll be able to eat dinner at night.

M: You can't just go to a restaurant or cook something?

W: I don't have money for that. Plus, my dorm doesn't have any cooking facilities.

M: Ah, yeah, that's a good point I hadn't considered.

W: There's something else I should mention. Think about how hungry you get during exam time. There are plenty of times that I could use a late-night snack, but there's nowhere to get any food. Now, I can walk to the building next door to my dorm and get a sandwich or something. I'm really pleased about that.

◆ **Sample Response**

The announcement concerns a change in the hours of operation of one of the cafeterias at the school. According to the announcement, the cafeteria will no longer close at 8:00 PM on weeknights but will instead stay open until midnight. It will remain open later on the weekend as well. The woman is pleased with the changes described in the announcement. First, she says that because of her classes and part-time job, she finishes after the dining halls are closed. As a result, she can't have dinner. But thanks to the extended hours, she will be able to eat now. The second reason she gives in support of this decision concerns exam time. She mentions that there are many occasions when she wants a snack late at night while studying. Unfortunately, she can't go anywhere to get food. Now, however, she'll be able to get some food just by walking to the building where the cafeteria is.

Task 3

Listening

Script 03-09

Professor: In almost every moment of our lives, we are learning something. A lot of times, we don't even realize that this is happening. Psychologists use the term latent learning to describe this process. Basically, this is when you gain knowledge but you don't use it until later when you need it. Let me give you an example to clarify.

Let's assume that you are a student who does not

have a car. So every day you ride to school in your friend's car, taking the same route to school each time. But one day, your friend is sick, so she can't drive you to school. You end up riding your bike to school. Since you have never had to go to school by yourself, you don't know the route exactly. But because you have ridden with your friend in the car so many times, you find that you actually do know how to get to the campus. You have no problem remembering where to turn and which roads to take.

This is a perfect example of latent learning. You acquired the knowledge of how to get to school but did not use this knowledge until you needed it.

◆ **Sample Response**

The professor begins his lecture by introducing the term latent learning. In the reading passage, latent learning is described as learning that occurs without a person realizing it. The knowledge is stored subconsciously and is not used until later when the person needs it. In the lecture, the instructor talks about this process in more detail. He talks about a student who rides to school every day in a friend's car. The student and her friend take the same route to school each day. One day, the student's friend is sick and cannot drive her to school, so the student has to go to school by herself. Although the student has never been taught the exact route to the school, she knows how to get there. This is due to latent learning. The student subconsciously learned where to turn and which roads to take on her way to school and is therefore able to get there by herself.

Task 4

Listening

Script 03-10

Professor: Have you ever noticed that each kind of product has a different package? Even the same product, like soap, comes in packages of several different shapes and materials. This isn't by mistake. When marketing teams design packages, they try to design something that has broad appeal.

Some packaging is designed to attract consumers. When people shop for products today, they tend to prefer products that are convenient and easy to use. You can see this with the evolution of ketchup bottle design. For many years, ketchup usually came in a glass container. It was easy to store and cheap to produce. But it wasn't very easy to use. Ketchup companies eventually realized this, so they switched over to flexible plastic bottles. These bottles are simple to use—you just have to squeeze them to get your ketchup—and they don't break easily like glass

containers can. And best of all, they don't cost any more than glass containers, meaning that ketchup prices have stayed the same.

Oh, package design should appeal to retailers, too. Think about prepackaged foods, such as cookies and potato chips. Now think about how these packages look. They use bright colors, strong lettering, and cartoon characters. In other words, these packages are highly noticeable. So what does this mean for retailers? Increased profits. These attractive boxes cause customers to spend more money when they shop, which means more money for stores. Retailers also like attractive packaging designs because they make their stores brighter and more colorful. This makes the stores nicer places to be in, which, again, motivates consumers to spend more money.

◆ **Sample Response**

The entire lecture is about the importance of a product's package design. The instructor points out that packaging must have broad appeal. She explains this concept in two ways. First, she says that some packaging works to attract customers. Today's consumers want products that are convenient and simple to use, and product makers have changed their designs to meet this demand. According to the professor, one of these products is ketchup bottles. Although ketchup used to come in glass bottles, today it comes in flexible plastic containers. Unlike glass containers, these are easy to use and do not break easily. Packaging should also appeal to retailers. The professor talks about prepackaged foods to explain this. She says that these foods come in brightly colored packages to make them more noticeable and to make stores nicer places to be in. This benefits retailers because it causes customers to spend more money when they shop.

TOEFL®
MAP
New TOEFL® Edition

Speaking

Intermediate